IMPROVISATIONAL ISLAM

Improvisational Islam

Indonesian Youth in a
Time of Possibility

Nur Amali Ibrahim

Cornell University Press
Ithaca and London

First published 2018 by Cornell University Press

Printed in the United States of America

Library of Congress Cataloging-in-Publication Data

Names: Ibrahim, Nur Amali, author.
Title: Improvisational Islam : Indonesian youth in a time of possibility / Nur Amali Ibrahim.
Description: Ithaca : Cornell University Press, 2018. | Includes bibliographical references and index.
Identifiers: LCCN 2018003313 (print) | LCCN 2018005722 (ebook) | ISBN 9781501727870 (e-book pdf) | ISBN 9781501727887 (e-book epub/mobi) | ISBN 9781501727856 | ISBN 9781501727856 (hardcover) | ISBN 9781501727863 (pbk.)
Subjects: LCSH: Muslim youth—Religious life—Indonesia—Jakarta. | Muslim college students—Religious life—Indonesia—Jakarta. | Islam—Indonesia—Jakarta—Customs and practices. | Universitas Islam Negeri Syarif Hidayatullah Jakarta—Students—Religion. | Universitas Indonesia—Students—Religion. | Ethnology—Indonesia—Jakarta.
Classification: LCC BP188.18.Y6 (ebook) | LCC BP188.18.Y6 I27 2018 (print) | DDC 297.084/209598—dc23
LC record available at https://lccn.loc.gov/2018003313

For my grandparents

CONTENTS

ACKNOWLEDGMENTS

I have accrued many debts over the past ten or so years that I worked on this project. First and foremost, I wish to thank the numerous student activists and civil society activists in Indonesia who generously shared their lives with me and taught me so much about what it means to lead a socially and politically engaged existence. My gratitude toward them is immeasurable. Even though I could never do full justice to their stories, I hope that the book is able to convey a small part of their hopes, dreams, and struggles. For facilitating my research and continually pointing me in the right direction, I am grateful to the staff at Center for the Study of Religion and Culture at the State Islamic University in Jakarta (UIN Syarif Hidayatullah), particularly Irfan Abubakar, Sholehudin Aziz, Amelia Fauzia, Idris Hemay, Mohammad Nabil, and Sylvia Nurman. Special thanks are also due to my Indonesian friends Wina Andreini, Nelden Djakababa, Tito Imanda, Veronika Kusumaryati, Subhan Muhammad, Ully Damari Putri, and Rianne Subijanto for their support and encouragement during my research and for teaching me invaluable lessons about Indonesia.

This project was initially conceived through discussions with my teachers and mentors at the Department of Anthropology, New York University. My adviser Michael Gilsenan has inspired me for many years with his intellectual vision and stamina and ability to view the world in oblique ways. Once, when I was paralyzed by the fear of having to produce something new in the research, he said that I should instead imagine that my task was to shift a prism ever so slightly such that the light can hit it at a different angle and become refracted ever more brightly. The advice, which helped make the writing less daunting, is an example of how instrumental his guidance has been to my work. Sally Merry's research on law, violence, and quantification has shaped my thinking in important ways, as has Faye Ginsburg's work on the politics of representation and the coproduction of disparate religious and political identities. I am also fortunate to have learned from other fantastic teachers like Bambi Schieffelin, Patricia Spyer, Emily Martin, Fred Myers, and Tom Beidelman. My graduate school compatriots Meghan Harrington, Hyejin Nah, Ram Natarajan, Pilar Rau, Louis Philippe Römer, Sandra Rozental, Stephanie Sadre-Orafai, Ayako Takamori, Sabra Thorner, Anna Wilking, and Emily Yates-Doerr made New York University a very special place for me and played crucial roles in the development of this project.

A number of institutions and individuals offered critical support to the project at its various stages. Fieldwork in Indonesia was funded by the National Science Foundation, the Social Science Research Council, the Wenner-Gren Foundation for Anthropological Research, and numerous grants from New York University, which also included a dissertation writing fellowship. The project developed further at Harvard University, where I received a postdoctoral fellowship at the Harvard Academy for International and Area Studies. I thank Jorge Domínguez, Kathleen Hoover, and Larry Winnie for their constant support and mentorship as the book started to take shape. With a stroke of luck, I found myself in the company of gifted scholars and sharp interlocutors like Anne Clément, Jesse Driscoll, Rachel Leow, Juno Parreñas, Caroline Schuster, Noah Tamarkin, and Nurfadzilah Yahaya as I wrote the book. Bara Arumugam and Noorindah Iskandar provided moral encouragement from afar. Harvard Academy generously organized an author's conference for me, where Brinkley Messick, Daromir Rudnyckyj, Gregory Starrett, and Mary Steedly gave incisive feedback on substantial portions of the manuscript.

As the project evolved, I was able to present it to many academic audiences, including at Cornell University (hosted by the Comparative Muslim Societies Program), Ohio State University (Department of Comparative Studies), the University of Cincinnati (Department of Anthropology), Yale University (Southeast Asian Studies Council), and the Social Science Research Council (Inter-Asian Connections conference in Hong Kong). I am grateful to the various communities of scholars and students for the stimulating conversations about my project. I have also benefited tremendously from the presentations that I have delivered at the annual meetings of the American Anthropological Association. In particular, I wish to thank John Bowen, Amira Mittermaier, and David Nugent for the indispensable advice they have given in their capacities as panel discussants.

I feel extraordinarily fortunate to have landed a job at the Departments of Religious Studies and International Studies, Indiana University, where I brought the project to its completion. Winnifred Sullivan offered instrumental support and fostered a vibrant intellectual environment. My colleagues and tireless advocates Keera Allendorf, Purnima Bose, Stephanie Deboer, Ilana Gershon, Seema Golestaneh, Kevin Jaques, Stephanie Kane, Padraic Kenney, Yan Long, and Phil Parnell provided friendship and solidarity as well as feedback that improved the book in the latter stages of its preparation. It was a real pleasure for me to work with Cornell University Press to bring this book into fruition. I thank the two anonymous reviewers who offered helpful comments and suggestions. I am especially grateful to my editor Jim Lance for his patience and enthusiasm over the project.

Throughout this entire journey, my family has been a constant source of love and support. I am forever grateful to my father, mother, and siblings for allowing me to do the work that I enjoy, even if that meant I had to live thousands of miles away from them. And because I am Southeast Asian, my aunties, uncles, and cousins have also been by my side along the way. My maternal grandparents, Adnan Salman and Som Ismail, died long before the book took on its nascent form, yet they were somehow always present in my writing process. Both my grandparents had a commitment to writing, even though neither of them were highly educated. My grandfather had a vintage typewriter that he loved, and he used it often to write personal letters and family histories. My grandmother, on the other hand, could not read or write. When she died, we were surprised to discover a book and a pencil under her pillow. She was teaching herself how to write by copying the names of days and months in an old appointment book. T-U-E-S-D-A-Y, T-U-E-S-D-A-Y, T-U-E-S-D-A-Y, she would write again and again, or F-E-B-R-U-A-R-Y, F-E-B-R-U-A-R-Y, F-E-B-R-U-A-R-Y. On those days that I struggled with my writing, I imagine the click! clack! ding! sounds of my grandfather at his typewriter and my grandmother scribbling one letter in front of the other, and I push on. The book is dedicated to their loving memory.

Improvisational Islam

PROLOGUE

At the encouragement of his peers, a twenty-year-old Indonesian under-graduate named Hassan stepped gingerly into a shallow basin that had been filled with shards of broken glass.[1] He was nervous about sustain-ing a bad cut, even though a small kitchen towel had been placed over the glass to prevent direct contact with the soles of his bare feet. "Don't worry," reassured a slightly older male student, whose role was to oversee the performance of this activity, "Allah will protect you." With a friend holding each of his hands, Hassan began to do a slow, stationary march in the basin, raising each leg such that the knee would reach his waist level, his eyes transfixed on the broken glass that crunched menacingly each time a foot came down on it. The older student shouted "Takbir!" an Ar-abic word conjoining Muslims to utter the name of God in times of both distress and celebration. "Allahu Akbar! God is Great!" was the unison response from the eight male undergraduates in the room, each of whom would have to take a turn stepping on the glass. After about two or three minutes that seemed like an eternity in his own estimation, Hassan was asked to step out. There were no lacerations, much to his relief, though a couple of his friends required bandages for the small cuts they received.

Later, Hassan asked me what I thought of the activity. "It was weird," I said. He just smiled. I had arrived in Indonesia's capital city Jakarta in 2008 to observe what had become of Islam since the nation became a secular democracy ten years earlier. For three decades from 1965 to 1998, Indonesia was ruled by the military authoritarian regime of President Suharto that heavily controlled public expressions of religiosity, permitting those that were compatible with state ideology while banning others that were regarded as threats. When Suharto's rule ended, wide-ranging democratic reforms were implemented in Indonesia as free and fair elections were held for the first time since 1955, provinces were given greater autonomy to pass their own bylaws, and press bans were lifted. Democracy's arrival on Indonesian shores helped to erode the limits that had been imposed on the religious imagination. Numerous new and previously marginalized religious actors appeared on the scene to demand inclusion in the emergent political landscape, and brought along with them new bodily operations that one could perform in order to be pious. I observed many such religious innovations over the course of the eighteen months that I conducted ethnographic research in Jakarta, including the glass-stepping activity that involved Hassan.

The activity was organized by the Campus Proselytization Association (Lembaga Dakwah Kampus), an Islamist student organization that Hassan joined the previous year. The activity's name, "A Session for Overcoming Your Fears" (Sesi menghilangkan rasa takut), describes not only its learning objectives but also hints at the ambitions that Islamists have in Indonesia. Islamists believe that Islam should be the guiding principle behind all domains of social organization, including politics, the law, and economics. Whereas the Suharto state banned Islamists from formal politics, democracy enabled them to take part in elections in order to bring their philosophy on religion into fruition. In addition to contesting for a share of state power, Islamists are also interested in influencing public opinion. They establish mosque study circles, charitable foundations, cooperatives for small business owners, clinics and hospitals, and schools offering education from kindergarten to high school as platforms for proselytization (*dakwah*). Islamists regard university students like Hassan as a core constituency of their movement. Student groups are thought of as places where youths are groomed into religiously observant cadres who will advance the Islamist cause in both spheres of formal and cultural politics. Participants in these student groups are exposed to a wide range of pedagogical and pietistic activities, including traipsing on broken glass, in order to inculcate the fortitude necessary to carry out the Islamist mission.

What intrigued me about the broken glass activity was not the aspect of bodily harm, as inflicting violence on the flesh is often integral to the rituals of religious practitioners, including Muslims like the Shi'as who flagellate themselves to commemorate the historical persecution of their community, or the Sufi mystics who impale themselves to attain an ecstatic union with God. Rather, it was the disclosure by Hassan that the activity had in fact been inspired by the American self-help guru Tony Robbins. Through books, lectures, and seminars that have soaring popularity especially in the business world, Robbins tells people that they hold the key to their personal success. One of Robbins's signature methods to cultivate the sense of individual agency requires participants to walk barefoot across hot coal while loudly chanting "Yes! Yes! Yes!" to gather courage. The exercise teaches participants to find inner strength to surmount the adversities life throws at them, whether it is a fire pit or a slumping economic climate or a personal health crisis. It is a method that Islamists have adopted with several modifications: replacing burning embers with broken glass, and shifting the goal from creating self-maximizing individuals to creating God-fearing, socially conscious religious adherents. What I found fascinating, therefore, was the sheer imaginativeness in the Islamists' enterprise, the borrowing from elsewhere in order to cultivate piety, in seeming contradiction to their frequent representation as rigid and conservative.

In addition to self-help, Islamists have also readily embraced other practices originating from the business world, from techniques of bureaucracy to corporate lingo and structures of hierarchy and promotion. One such example, which Hassan showed me one day, was a pocket-size accounting book that had been given to each member in the student organization. Instead of tracking income and expenditures, however, the accounting book was used for monitoring the number of times each person prays, fasts, and reads the Quran. Hassan's responsibility was to document the ritual practices he performed on a daily basis. At the end of every week, the book will be checked by a more senior student to determine whether satisfactory quantities of pious rituals have been attained. If found to be a laggard, Hassan could be subjected to various kinds of disciplinary action, especially shaming. At the end of the year, the numbers will be tabulated to arrive at a numerical representation of his religious devotion. Theoretically, the greater the devotional indicator, the higher the rank he can occupy in the student organization. This system reveals a central premise of the Islamist mission, which is that relegating political leadership to the pious is necessary for the spiritual transformation of Indonesian society. In order for this plan to materialize, Islamists will have to trust that the use of hybrid methods adapted from business practices, like the piety accounting book and the broken-glass activity, can actually result in the successful accomplishment of religious aims.

I asked Hassan and his friends how they got the idea to incorporate Western business practices into their religious activities. "Kita coba-coba aja," they responded. We're just trying it out.

Apart from the Islamists, other Muslim groups were also experimenting with Western ideas and concepts in their attempts to gain political legitimacy in democratic Indonesia. My fieldwork led me to a group of Muslims who call themselves "liberal" and who position themselves as the ideological rivals of the Islamists. Liberal Muslims are influenced by key principles of secular liberalism like freedom, pluralism, tolerance, and equality, believing that these values lie at the heart of Islam. Rejecting the Islamist dogma that God's commandments should be implemented in their totality, liberal Muslims point out that Islamists are in fact conflating two separate issues: the first being divinely revealed scripture, which is sacred and unalterable; the second, human interpretation of scripture, which is fallible and therefore changeable. In other words, liberals want to make a distinction between the letter of the law and the spirit of the law. Liberals advocate for the practice of Islamic law that takes into account the historical and cultural variations in the lives of its adherents, which means that religious laws implemented in Arab societies, for example, will not necessarily be appropriate in the Indonesian context. It is only when such nuances are taken into account, liberals believe, can religion be the liberating force it is supposed to be and uplift the human condition. Like the Islamists, liberal Muslims hope to present a persuasive case in the court of public opinion. They work largely within the ambit of civil society, reaching out to their audience through radio talk shows, books and periodicals, and lectures and seminars.

Liberals believe that their religious outlook will materialize only when new reading habits are nurtured. A focal point of their activism is university campuses, because liberals share the Islamist view of students as assets of paramount importance. The most famous liberal Muslim student organization in Jakarta and perhaps also nationally is Formaci (an acronym for Forum Mahasiswa Ciputat, or the Ciputat Undergraduates Forum, Ciputat being the name of the district in which it is located), which was where I observed male and female undergraduates reading and discussing books. All of Formaci's participants have spent their entire lives in religious educational settings, but none of their meetings were devoted to the study of Islamic scriptures. Instead, like students in a Western civilization course in American or European universities, they read the "great books" in the humanities and social sciences. During my first visit to the group's main office, I noticed a whiteboard that had the schedule of readings for their twice-weekly meetings. Plato, Aristotle, Locke, Hume, Kant, Hegel, Marx, Nietzsche, Heidegger, and Habermas were some of the thinkers whose works the students were planning to read over the next few weeks. The students, however, have not completely lost interest in Islamic scriptures. Rather, the humanities and social sciences were regarded as a necessary detour in order to approach the scriptures with fresh eyes and from different points of view.

The detour seems to involve behaving in ways that are unorthodox in Islamic standards. "Quickly! Close the door behind me!" exclaimed a male undergraduate named Rizal as he burst into Formaci's office. He had a small plastic bag of *gorengan*, an assortment of fried dough commonly sold by street vendors in Indonesia as an afternoon snack, and promptly passed it around the room. It was the Muslim holy month of Ramadan, when religious adherents would fast from sunrise to sunset, yet most of the twelve participants in the room were eating in broad daylight. Rizal informed me later that few students in Formaci were religiously observant. Most stopped praying and fasting after joining the liberal Muslim group and reading humanistic and social scientific literature on a regular basis. In Rizal's succinct words, "When you keep reading about how religion is a social construct, you're not that interested in worship." Despite the apparent lack of interest in religious rituals, students like Rizal remained committed to religious debates to promote interpretations of Islam that often diverge from traditional beliefs or Islamist doctrines. This suggests that their refusal to pray or fast is not simply laziness or religious apathy, but rather the active cultivation of a particular type of ethical disposition—impiety. Impiety allows liberal Muslims to gain distance from the religion so that they can criticize aspects of its practice that they regard as outmoded or coercive. In other words, they were trying to disengage from religion in order to reengage with it.

This book is about novel and unexpected ways of being Muslim, where religious dispositions are achieved through techniques that have little or no precedent in classical Islamic texts or concepts. It is partly a story about Indonesia, where the removal of constraints imposed by an authoritarian regime has opened up the imaginative terrain, allowing particular types of religious beliefs and practices to emerge. At the same time, I would suggest that the Indonesian case study, which occurs in a heightened and volatile political context, brings into sharper relief processes that are happening in ordinary Muslim life everywhere. To be a practitioner of their religion, Muslims draw on and are inspired by not only their holy scriptures, but also the nontraditional ideas and practices that circulate in their society, which importantly include those that originate in the West. In the contemporary Western political discourse where Muslims are often portrayed as uncompromising and adversarial to the West and where bans and walls are deemed necessary to keep them out, this story about flexible and creative Muslims is an important one to tell.

Introduction

"Improvisational Islam" is the term I will use to describe the unconventional forms of religious practices I observed in Indonesia, such as behaving impiously and reading humanistic and social scientific books in order to rethink religion, and using techniques of accounting and stepping on broken glass to develop religious fervor. Improvisation is acting, performing, or making something spontaneously using whatever resources that are available, often as a response to a situation that is rapidly changing. It is an important part of cultural activity (Hallam and Ingold 2007). A jazz singer creates a new melody on the spot to fit the chord progression of a song; a stand-up comedian comes up with a witty comeback to a heckler; improv theater actors make up the plot and dialogue of their performance based on the audience's suggestion; a rapper freestyles lyrics to out-brag and out-insult verbal opponents in battle raps. Improvisation occurs outside of the arts too. In her study of an oncology ward in Botswana, Julie Livingston (2012) discovers that doctors, whose professional ethics demand that they practice methodically and deliberately, dispense medical treatment using experimentation and trial and error when they are faced with dire shortages of medicine and other essential supplies.

As in these cultural arenas, improvisation is also an important part of religion. However, this is seldom acknowledged in public discourses on religion. In the West, politicians, policy makers, and commentators on religion, influenced by their familiarity with textual forms of Christianity and guided by the secular assumption that religion exists separately from other spheres like politics, often assume that religion is tied only to authoritative religious scriptures. Thus, ongoing Western attempts to understand "Islamic" terrorism have tended to focus on the content of the Quran and on how Muslims pray, fast, and perform other ritual obligations (Abu-Lughod 2013; Mamdani 2004). These efforts assume that religious scriptures and rituals themselves, divorced from context or interpretation, could offer valuable insights about Islam or why terror occurs. Religious believers, of course, seldom follow scriptures or doctrines to the letter or completely defer to the authority of their religious elites. Instead, religious believers understand scriptures and doctrines creatively in relation to the circumstances and exigencies of their everyday lives, and are dialectically shaped by the contexts in which they live at the same time they are making these societies through their religiously inspired actions. As religion is always contingent upon context and culture, it is always, to quote Robert Orsi (2012, 150–51), "improvised and situational."

The religious improvisation I observed in Indonesia has produced hybrid forms of religious practices, or what Aihwa Ong and Stephen Collier call "global assemblages," which are "the product of multiple determinations that are not reducible to a single logic" (2005, 12). An example of such global assemblages is the piety accounting notebook, which draws on Western bureaucratic ideals of accounting and accountability but which has been repurposed to cultivate Islamic piety. When I describe the composite character of these Indonesian religious forms, I am not referring to "syncretism," a concept that has a long history in the study of Islam in Southeast Asia. Clifford Geertz is perhaps the most prominent representative of this scholarly approach. Geertz argues that when Islam arrived in Southeast Asia in the fourteenth century, it did not move into "an essentially virgin area" but rather into "one of Asia's greatest political, aesthetic, religious, and social creations, the Hindu-Buddhist Javanese state" (1968, 11). As such, Southeast Asian Islam developed a syncretic character where orthodox beliefs and practices get mixed up with Indic ideas of ghosts, gods, jinns, and prophets. Syncretism has been offered as an explanation for the widely celebrated pragmatism, flexibility, and tolerance of Southeast Asian Islam—but it also problematically suggests that when it is not influenced by Hinduism and Buddhism, Islam is emphatic, exclusivist, and rigid.

By foregrounding the part-Western, part-Islamic global assemblages that are formed through religious improvisation, I am responding to the way Western public discourses consistently represent Islam as incompatible with the West. Such representations, as Edward Said argued in his classic study on Orientalism (1979), became pervasive during the colonization of Muslim lands by European nations at around the eighteenth century. I am especially concerned with how Islam relates to the values of Western liberalism that have a genealogy extending back to the Age of Enlightenment, with such strands as freedom, equality, individual agency, individual rights, women's rights, democratic citizenship, and rationality. Popular Western imagination tends to locate Islam, with its supposed proclivity for oppression, intolerance, misogyny, homophobia, and authoritarianism, as standing outside of liberalism (Massad 2015). This is all too evident in the controversies over the publication of cartoon images of the Prophet Muhammad in the Danish newspaper *Jyllands-Posten* in 2006 and the French magazine *Charlie Hebdo* in 2015. When Muslims took offense at those images, many Westerners wondered why Muslims did not respect freedom of speech or have a sense of humor about their religion. Incidents like these fortify the image of Muslims as alien and contribute to the systematic exclusion of Muslims from Western societies, including turning away refugees feeling from war-torn Middle Eastern and North African nations.

Some anthropologists have responded to these issues by writing about Islam from the "self-cultivation" approach, which examines how Muslims impose discipline on themselves to become faithful adherents of Islam. The approach is popularized by the studies by Saba Mahmood (2005) and Charles Hirschkind (2006) on conservative Islamists in Egypt, the former focusing on women who attend religious study circles in mosques, the latter on men who listen to religious sermons on cassette tapes. Broadly speaking, the approach shows that the standards and parameters set by Western modernity do not necessarily define how Muslims behave, given that they are subjected to different modalities of power. Whereas Western secular liberals are informed by Enlightenment ideals of individual freedom, Muslims are guided by the authoritative scriptures and doctrines in their religion. Mahmood's interlocutors, for example, draw on traditional concepts such as shyness and modesty to achieve self-discipline and become pious Muslim women. Mahmood explains that the women's behavior should not be seen as an expression of feminist agency, commonly understood by Western scholars as the capacity to pursue one's individual interests in the face of pressures from custom, tradition, and religion. Instead, the women's activities are created jointly by their individual wills and their religion. Agency, therefore, belongs both to the women and the Islamic system of belief and practices in which the women are located.

Though Mahmood and Hirschkind have crucially argued that liberal values do not always denote what practices are deemed appropriate, they have also inadvertently drawn an overly stark divide between Islam and the secular liberal West, reinforcing the Orientalist binary that Edward Said worked so hard to expose. The problem is that Mahmood and Hirschkind conceived of their respective research projects rather narrowly, by focusing on one particular type of Muslim (conservative Islamists) and one particular type of religious socialization (how these Muslims draw on classical Islamic texts, concepts, and doctrines). Diversity among Muslims is under-theorized. There is, as Amira Mittermaier (2010) points out, "too little Islam" in Mahmood's and Hirschkind's anthropology of Islam.[1] During my time in Indonesia, I have learned that Muslim piety can be grounded as much in a tradition that stands resolutely other to the West as in modern and liberal techniques. Western methods are taken up not only by liberal Muslims, who combine a lifelong education in Islamic schools with a voracious appetite to learn from humanistic and social scientific literature, but also by conservative Islamists, who read Tony Robbins and draw on rationalized bureaucratic techniques to enact a puritanical model of piety. In my work, the binary between Islam and Western secular liberalism dissolves.

An important question to consider is why Muslims adopt modern and liberal techniques in their religious practices. This is because they live in a world that is saturated with Western liberal ideals and thus improvise and adjust their religious practices accordingly. Although Indonesians have debated for at least the past century how to be both Muslims and modern,[2] these discussions have intensified since the fall of President Suharto's New Order regime in 1998. The New Order came into power in 1965 by overthrowing a left-leaning incumbent government and massacring at least half a million people accused of being Communists, extraordinary acts of violence that were supported by the United States in its global efforts to curb the ideological influence of the Soviet Union. The New Order remained in power for thirty-two mostly unopposed years: internationally, it cultivated the support of Western nations and corporations; domestically, it kept citizens docile by terrorizing them. The regime's eventual collapse was followed by the implementation of democratic and neoliberal reforms with the assistance of Western nations and international governance organizations. In this context, there was an enlargement of Western liberal ideals in Indonesian society as issues like human rights, gender equality, transparency, citizenship, accountability, self-help, and free enterprise occupied center stage in public discourses.

When I arrived in Indonesia for research in 2008, the liberal Muslims and the conservative Islamists, just two of the multiple factions competing for influence in post–New Order Indonesia, had already begun to incorporate liberal ideas and practices in their respective models for national spiritual healing. Their embrace of liberalism could be understood as an assent to the West and the ideals it promotes, despite how deeply complicit the West was in the harms inflicted on ordinary Indonesians by the New Order. This is not a story about Muslims who are hell-bent on opposing and destroying the West, nor is it one about the West as the natural home of freedom, ingenuity, and all that is good about the world, or Islam as the natural home of intolerance, rigidity, and all that is bad about the world. Such narratives are based on a gross misrecognition and misrepresentation of the dynamics of power in contemporary geopolitics. Instead, this is a story about the hard creative labor that Muslims put in to cope with the continuing hegemony of the West. They do so through religious improvisation, the trial-and-error attempts to adapt their religion to changing circumstances, thus revealing the heterogeneous, flexible, and enlightened qualities of Islam.

A Time of Possibility

I devoted much effort, at the beginning of fieldwork, toward gathering information on the families of the youths of this study, hoping that kinship could shed important light on the youths' religiously improvisational activities. Much to my disappointment, my interlocutors seldom shared my enthusiasm about cognates and affines, and typically provided banal and seemingly uninsightful responses to my questions about their families. Hassan, the student in the conservative Islamist organization, pithily described his parents as "normal people" (*orang biasa*). When I asked him to elaborate on their supposed normalcy, he replied that there was nothing unusual or interesting about his parents' lives. They were low-ranking civil servants in Sumatra (his mother was a teacher, while his father worked for the municipal government) who provided a comfortable though far from extravagant life for their three children. They observed their Islamic rituals but were not overly concerned with long-standing modernist-versus-traditionalist debates regarding the correct forms of Islamic practice. Political topics were allegedly nonexistent in family conversations, except when the elections came around. Hassan's rather dismissive characterization of his parents was perhaps his way of telling me that I was looking at the wrong places if I wanted to understand his activism. It was not his parents who provided him with political education; rather, it was the fictive kin in activist circles, his contemporaries whom he met in university and about whom he was unmistakably more loquacious.

While I would eventually follow Hassan's cue and examine the influence of his activist fictive kin, I also came to realize that his descriptions of his parents were in fact more sociologically illuminating than I had originally assumed. Hassan's stories portrayed a generational divide between the lives his parents led (normal, boring, apolitical) and the lives that he and his contemporaries lived (extraordinary, exciting, political). By "generational," I am invoking Karl Mannheim's use of the term that refers less to age stratification than to a shared world that is identified with a specific set of social and historical conditions. "The fact that people are born at the same time, or that their youth, adulthood and old age coincide, does not in itself involve similarity of location [in the social and historical process]," Mannheim says. "What does create a similar location is that they are in a position to experience the same events and data" (Mannheim 1952, 388). Alternatively, one could also use Émile Durkheim's ([1912] 1995) analytical vocabulary and say that Hassan and his parents belonged to different "social times." For Durkheim, time is experienced primarily in relation to collective social activity, whereas time in nature is important only as a reference point for people to analyze and understand time spent

socially. Mannheim's and Durkheim's focus on temporal divisions resulting from social and historical circumstances have helped me understand
that the particular forms of religious improvisation I observed are possible
only for people who are part of a particular generation and live in a particular social time. I call this the time of possibility.

Hassan and his Indonesian contemporaries will have discovered that
they can express their political and religious opinions in a wide range of
ways. There are numerous political parties they can support (in 2014,
there were about two dozen active ones). Whether they are anti-Christian,
antigay, anti-Islamic-hard-liners, antipornography, pro-Palestine, pro–
women's rights, pro-environmentalism, or pro-religious pluralism, they
can participate in the street protests that have become ubiquitous in major
Indonesian cities. Many of these street protests are also targeted at government failures—for example, its inability to eradicate corruption or keep
gas prices down—though young Indonesians, who are among the world's
largest Internet users, are increasingly expressing dissent by sending angry
messages to the Facebook or Twitter accounts of politicians and suffer no
bigger consequence than getting "blocked." These young persons could
go to bookstores, either chain bookstores located in big shopping malls
or small specialty ones located around university campuses, and purchase
a vast spectrum of publications on Islam, from the writings of Islamist
thinkers like the Pakistani Abul Al'a Maududi to those of progressive
reformers like the Egyptian Muhammad Abduh. It may occur to them
that the local publishing industry is flourishing, given that many books
once regarded by the state as subversive, like Karl Marx's *Das Kapital*
and Adolf Hitler's *Mein Kampf*, are no longer banned. They can debate
these books in study circles that meet in the corridors, cafeterias, or prayer
rooms of university campuses, and think dangerous thoughts. All this is
possible because the time in which they lived permitted spontaneous acts,
risk taking, and high passions.

Times were different just a generation earlier, the generation of Hassan's parents, who spent most of their lives under the New Order. When
Suharto came to power, he promised political stability and economic
development to a young nation rocked by factional divides among the
political elites, by separatist movements, hyperinflation, and widespread
famine. Suharto restored order through the often violent suppression of
threats to that order. In 1974, for example, at the occasion of a state visit

by the Japanese prime minister Kakuei Tanaka, hundreds of student activists were arrested for holding demonstrations in Jakarta criticizing how the state's liberal economic policies benefited only Suharto's cronies. In 1979, following student criticism of state corruption that culminated in the demand for Suharto's impeachment, the state implemented a set of policies known as the NKK/BKK (Normalization of Campus Life / Bodies for the Coordination of Student Affairs) designed to depoliticize universities. Subsequently, student publications and political activities were banned. Student leaders were stripped of their positions and replaced with those selected by campus administration. To redirect student focus from politics to academics, the minimum number of course credits per semester was increased. Similar forms of discipline were imposed on other groups that openly displayed disobedience. In the 1980s, street criminals were shot by "mysterious assassins" and left to die in public as part of a state policy to deter crime. Until mass Muslim organizations declared a commitment to secular nationalism over Islamism in 1984, religious leaders critical of the New Order were routinely tortured and imprisoned.[3]

The use of terror and violence as techniques of rule meant that the New Order was able to create political stasis, a time of suspended animation that was contrary to what Hassan and his peers would know. In his masterly study of political repression under the New Order, John Pemberton (1994) examines how stasis was attained during elections (which were organized every five years). During each campaigning season, there would inevitably be rumors floating around, stories about sinister incidents that might happen and jeopardize the electoral process. Yet, Pemberton observes, such incidents were always thoroughly anticipated by the government and quashed before they could materialize. By election day, the much-rumored threats seemed to dissipate, allowing the elections to proceed smoothly. As usual, the elections concluded with a convincing victory by the state party, Golkar. The elections were undoubtedly rigged, but more important, they were public displays of the state's ability to maintain an appearance of security and stability. The New Order's success in creating the sense of a place where nothing ever happens, Pemberton suggests, can be measured by Indonesia's relative invisibility in the international media, unusual for the fourth-most-populous nation in the world.

On May 21, 1998, Suharto stepped down from office. The Asian financial crisis of 1997, which brought soaring unemployment, inflation, and bankruptcies to Indonesia, spurred nationwide protests against "KKN," the popular abbreviation for the "corruption, collusion, and nepotism" that were entrenched in the New Order. Mere days before Suharto's resignation, thousands of students occupied the People's Consultative Assembly building in Jakarta while riots, looting, and rapes broke out in neighborhoods with large concentrations of ethnic Chinese (who were perceived as the primary beneficiaries of Suharto's economic policies), forcing the New Order to concede that it could no longer offer security and stability to the nation. Although the New Order did not simply disappear with Suharto's ouster—Golkar, the army, and other members of the political and economic elites that were close to Suharto remained powerful—there was a palpable sense that a new dawn for political expression and agency had arrived. Free and fair elections commenced in 1999. Five different people have become president in the two decades following Suharto's resignation, a consequence not only of the emerging and highly competitive multiparty democratic system, but also of reforms that limit the presidency to two five-year terms. New freedoms of the press and the proliferation of civil society organizations facilitated lively debates about the nation's past and future. Timor-Leste voted for independence in 2002, and the West Papuan and Acehnese separatist movements gained strength, while other provinces demanded autonomy to pass bylaws independently of Jakarta's authority.

New social types emerged in this context.[4] Many were proponents of what Lara Deeb (2006) calls "publicly engaged religiosity," in the sense that they had religious identities and activist causes and thus collapsed the separation between private religiosity and public politics that Suharto jealously guarded during most of his rule. These groups are a culmination of the religious awakening that Muslims in Indonesia (like their brethren in other parts of the Muslim world) have experienced since the 1990s, where there has been an unprecedented engagement with religious texts by Muslims who were not necessarily educated at Islamic religious institutions. There are marked differences among these groups in terms of their conception of Islam's public role. First to arrive on the scene were Islamist groups influenced by radical Salafi and Wahhabi ideologies that resorted to violence and vigilantism to implement "the sharia law" (which they took to mean the suppression of vice, including the prohibition of the sale of alcohol and the forced veiling of women); many of these groups have since been dismantled by the state.[5] Importantly, however, not all Islamists supported terror tactics. In contrast to the radicals, Islamists influenced by politically moderate factions of the Muslim Brotherhood believed that the implementation of Islamic law should occur through the democratic process. To this end, moderate Islamists established the Prosperous Justice Party (Partai Keadilan Sejahtera) in 1999, which has become one of Indonesia's leading parties as well as the major conservative voice in the legislature, and various civil society organizations that promote the movement's ideology. Hassan and his friends in the Campus Proselytization Association were affiliated with this network of moderate Islamist groups.

Despite their political successes, Islamists have encountered fierce opposition from Muslim civil society groups that support religious pluralism and deny the concept of a monolithic Islamic state or Islamic law. Some of the more prominent groups to have emerged after 1998 include the Liberal Islam Network, the Freedom Institute, the Setara Institute for Democracy and Peace, the Maarif Institute for Culture and Humanity, and the National Alliance for the Freedom of Religion and Faith—to which Rizal and his friends in the student association Formaci were affiliated. In his important study on Muslim participation in Indonesian democratization, Robert Hefner (2000) uses the label "civil Islam" to describe such groups (though my interlocutors prefer to call themselves "liberal"). The singular contribution of Hefner's work is that it demonstrates a robust Muslim commitment to democratic and civic ideals, thus debunking Samuel Huntington's (1996) flawed but influential "clash of civilizations" thesis. However, Hefner problematically suggests that Islam is essentially pluralist, that civil Islam is more legitimate than conservative Islam, and that Islamism "ignores the lessons of Muslim history" (20). What is considered to be "correct" or "proper" Islam is not inherent or already existing; rather, it is determined through the contests that pit believers with divergent interpretations of their religion.

A useful way of understanding Hefner's promotion of civil Islam as the true face of Islam is perhaps to see his work as a product of an increased global concern for Islam that began with the Taliban's takeover of Afghanistan in 1996 and which accelerated further with the 9/11 attacks. As an explicitly anti-Islam discourse linking the religion to violence became popular in this context, scholars concerned with challenging such essentialisms began to highlight moderate interpretations of Islam.[6] Hefner's work not only showcases Islamic moderation but also makes a case for the importance of Indonesia in this regard. "Some 88 percent of this nation's 210 million people officially profess Islam," he says. "On these grounds alone, what Indonesian Muslims think and do should be a matter of general interest. An investigation of Muslim politics in this tropical milieu, however, has another benefit. It allows us to distinguish features of Muslim politics that owe more to Middle Eastern circumstances than Islamic civilization as a whole. Marginalized in treatments of classical Islam, Indonesia must be central to any effort to come to terms with the diversity of modern Muslim politics" (6). The notion of Indonesia as home to Islamic moderation has also been promoted by political leaders eager to find an alternative to "bad" Muslim countries in the Middle East. In 2015, repeating a sentiment that he has expressed throughout his presidency, Barack Obama said that "Indonesia . . . is uniquely positioned to be able to help spread a message of peace and cooperation and modernity within the Muslim world."[7]

In short, Indonesia's democratic turn has seen the emergence of multiple attempts to define what Islam in Indonesia is, or ought to be. Islamist, liberal Muslim, and a whole host of other groups that appeared in this context are trying to convince the public that their respective model of the religion is the correct one. Scholars and political leaders seek to identify benevolent actors and organizations that should represent the moderate face of Islam. But the Islam that exists at the everyday level, the Islam associated with Hassan and Rizal that has resulted in practices like walking on broken glass or reading Hegel alongside the Quran, appears to be less circumscribed: it is tentative, experimental, and spills into multiple domains of social life. Yet these improvised attempts to reconcile Islamic and secular liberal values are also implicated in the contests to define who is the most Muslim of all. Improvisational Islam, therefore, not only stands in contrast to efforts to affix and assign particular characteristics to Islam, but is also deeply entangled with them, at once influencing and influenced by them.

Political and Playful Youths

Youths are the key agents of religious improvisation in Indonesia. Since the time students mobilized in large-scale demonstrations that helped to overthrow the Suharto regime in 1998, university campuses have been buzzing with political activity. Walk around the campus grounds of large state universities, as I often did, and you will invariably find students immersed in preparations for various kinds of activist projects, whether it is campaigning on behalf of political parties, protesting the university administration for raising tuition fees, protesting at the Malaysian or Saudi embassies for the ill-treatment of Indonesian migrant workers in those nations, or organizing conferences and film screenings to discuss various pertinent contemporary issues, to name just a few examples that I observed during fieldwork. I was amazed by how much time students invested in activism, often at the expense of their coursework. While most Indonesian students complete their bachelor's degree within four or five years, Rizal (the liberal Muslim student) was in his ninth year as an undergraduate when I first got to know him in 2008. He took fewer courses per semester than other students, not only because he was busy with student activism, but also because he had been working part-time in several liberal Muslim nongovernmental organizations. At long last, in his tenth year as an undergraduate, when his academic dean refused to extend his matriculation any further, Rizal completed all his course requirements, submitted his senior thesis, and received his degree. Such observations led me to investigate why student activists were so devoted to political causes.

Youth political agency has been the subject of many studies in recent years, spurred partly by the extraordinary Arab Spring protests that brought about regime changes in several Middle Eastern and North African nations. Many scholars discussed youth political agency in relation to the neoliberalization of the global economy that began in the 1970s and 1980s. As explained by David Harvey (2005), neoliberalism is a theory of political economy that proposes that human well-being can best be advanced through the free market. An implication of this theory is that the state should scale back on its economic interventions in order to allow the market to work naturally to set prices. The widespread adoption of neoliberal principles, however, has resulted in numerous social problems, including increases in corporate power, widening income gaps, declines in welfare programs, and job loss through downsizing. Across cultural contexts, scholars have discovered that youths are becoming increasingly frustrated by their simultaneous inclusion and exclusion from the neoliberal economy, as they are courted for their purchasing power but denied the opportunity to earn stable incomes despite advanced educational qualifications. Many of these economically precarious youths subsequently turn to media, particularly but not limited to contemporary digital technologies, as means for finding communities of support and making plans for response and mobilization.[8]

Indonesian student activism similarly reflects these global trends. Following the 1997 financial crisis, newspapers estimated that as many as four hundred thousand Indonesian students were unable to pay their tuition fees with the rapid proliferation of unemployment and bankruptcies. As students mobilized in the massive anti-Suharto protests in 1997–1998, they criticized the state's neoliberal economic policies for benefiting Suharto's immediate family members and cronies but not the general population. Karen Strassler (2010) observes the important role photography played in these demonstrations. Photographs of the demonstrations taken by protesters as personal souvenirs acquired a different meaning as they began to circulate among a wider student population. Taken from the vantage point of the protesters, the photographs brought the viewers into the middle of the action and allowed them to imagine and recognize themselves as important political actors, a process that Strassler calls "refracted visions." Not only did these photographs help to escalate student participation in the Suharto protests; they also cultivated the image of students as important witnesses to Indonesian political reform.

Another important factor driving Indonesian student activism is that Indonesian nationalism is founded on the myth of youth political agency. Enshrined historical narratives attribute the arousal of nationalist sentiment to a youth congress in 1928, which brought together representatives from different ethnic groups and political movements who were educated in colonial schools. After two days of discussing the prospect of independence from the Dutch, the participants closed the congress by reciting the Youth Pledge (Sumpah Pemuda), an oath of allegiance to one nation (Indonesia), one homeland (the land of Indonesia), and one language (Indonesian). A newly composed song titled "Indonesia Raya" (Prosper Indonesia) was performed on the violin. During the time of intense anticolonial struggle to secure independence, a period named the Indonesian Revolution (1945–1949), the 1928 youth congress became a constant reference in political rhetoric inciting youths to take up arms in the name of the nation. After the republic was established in 1949, "Indonesia Raya" became the national anthem, and Youth Pledge Day was commemorated by schoolchildren annually. In the 1970s, however, the connections between youth and nationalism were dismantled as Suharto sought to discipline student protesters. The regime began to refer to young people not as *pemuda* (political youth), but as *remaja* (teens), whose main interest was supposedly consumerism rather than politics. Suharto's removal from power thus allowed for the revival of what Doreen Lee (2016) calls "pemuda fever" in university campuses.

My research on the post–New Order rejuvenation of political consciousness was conducted in two student organizations, the Campus Proselytization Association and Formaci, where students learn about how to be Islamists and liberal Muslims respectively. I found it impossible to obtain precise membership numbers, given the revolving door allowing students to move from organization to organization in search of suitable activist causes. In fact, it was the constant movement among the student body that enabled me to move around and research rival ideological groups simultaneously. Nevertheless, the number of core participants in both groups was tiny (fewer than two hundred for the Campus Proselytization Association and fifty for Formaci), especially considering that Indonesian state universities have on average between thirty thousand and fifty thousand students. Yet statistical minuteness should not be confused with political insignificance, as small numbers of activists in Indonesia have historically been able to rouse the masses. Both groups are mixed-gender but strive to attract more female participants. Although activism is traditionally masculine, recent developments (such as improvements in women's education resulting in an equitable ratio of male-to-female undergraduates, the rise of the feminist movement, and the decline of the Suharto-era glorification of the domestic woman) have resulted in a growing recognition of young women's political agency.

Indonesians like to use the Dutch word *onderbouw* (meaning foundation or substructure) to describe the close relationship between the student movement and mass political movements in the nation. It is an appropriate characterization of my interlocutors, who are given mentoring, financial support, and career opportunities from the leading Islamist and liberal Muslim figures in the nation. These relationships are crucial in helping students acquire the correct resources to become Islamists and liberal Muslims. Rizal told me that he regarded liberal Islam as blasphemous when he initially encountered it, because its arguments sounded too Western and not Muslim enough. Over the course of his participation in Formaci, he was not only convinced by the ideals of liberal Islam but also became deeply committed to its realization. Rizal's transformation was recognized by people he called his "seniors" (he used the English word), or activists in a prominent liberal Muslim research center who were themselves previously student activists. When he graduated with his bachelor's degree, he was promptly offered a full-time research position where he headed the editorial team for one of its publications. His experience suggests that student activism is a form of what Jean Lave and Étienne Wenger (1991) call "legitimate peripheral participation," meaning that student activists are newcomers to the activities associated with a particular community of practice, the mastery of which will move them toward a fuller participation in that community.

Although the seniors play crucial roles in the acquisition of religious beliefs and practices, the process is not overly determined by them. The pedagogy in student organizations is largely autodidactic, which means that participants read and discuss texts on their own and without the supervision of pedagogical authorities like religious teachers, political leaders, or university professors. Autodidactic religious pedagogy became widespread in the Muslim world following the advent of print technology and mass literacy at the turn of the twentieth century, and has further accelerated since the Islamic revival of the 1980s (Eickelman and Piscatori 1996). Prior to these advances, Muslims were subjected to the authority of religious teachers who monopolized the interpretation of Islam's scriptures and hence determined what counts as orthodox beliefs and practices. When religiously unlettered Muslims gained unmediated access to religious texts, they were able to free themselves from what Jacques Rancière (1991) calls the "explication" by their teachers and attain "emancipation" from established hierarchies of knowledge perpetuated by the formal educational system. New religious interpretations by people proclaiming themselves to be religious authorities emerged as a result. Autonomous reading circles like the Campus Proselytization Association and Formaci hence present an opportunity for their participants to challenge, modify, and subvert authoritative religious knowledge—in other words, to be improvisational.

These student organizations, to put it differently, are playful spaces that permit the emergence of unusual and nontraditional forms of piety. By playful, I am referring not only to the pursuit of fun, which is important in youth culture,[9] but also to Johan Huizinga's sense of the term. For Huizinga, play is that space outside "real" life that allows people to enact their idealized notions of society, which can then dialectically reshape "real" life. Play can take various forms, such as religious rituals, poetry, and art. What is particularly interesting for my purposes is Huizinga's identification of the university as an important location where play occurs, suggesting that the Latin etymology of the word "campus" means "playground" (1950, 48). Huizinga's formulation of play encourages me to examine the impact that youthful religious improvisation can have on religion and politics in contemporary Indonesia. My aim, in contrast to that of other scholars of Islam who have focused largely on religious leaders who are middle-aged or elderly—like the mufti who provides fatwa for ordinary believers, or the Sufi sheikh who leads devotees to the path of spiritual enlightenment, or the Islamic judge who passes rulings in courts—is to consider the role of youths as important religious cultural brokers.

My study of female and male youths who are playfully and politically improvising with Islam hopes to continue the work that anthropologists of religion have done to unsettle the familiar ways of mapping society. Much of contemporary scholarship and popular commentaries on religion are still informed by the public-versus-private and religion-versus-secularism binaries, and, in the case of Islam, its binary division with Western liberalism.[10] Furthermore, these binaries are inflected with strong age and gender biases—the role of the young in public life, for example, is often underappreciated, and women are widely regarded as repressed in Islam compared to their peers in the West. But if we cling to the notion that religion (or a particular religious tradition) has particular characteristics and occupies particular spaces in society, we will never be able to obtain a good understanding of the lives and concerns of religious believers. It is only by releasing religion from the neat conceptual boxes where it has been sequestered, and examining how it mediates the encounter between people, their ambitions and insecurities, and the continually shifting contexts where they live, that we will be able to grasp the things that matter most in a religious world.

Surprised by Islam

The theoretical approach I take in this book shares common ground with the approach of scholars writing about "everyday Islam." In part writing against the "self-cultivation" approach discussed earlier, scholars concerned with everyday religion examine how Muslims are disciplined not only by the authoritative scriptures and doctrines in their religion, but by a multitude of religious and nonreligious concerns that are often tangled up together in complicated ways.[11] Samuli Schielke (2015), for example, describes the lives of youths in Egypt who want to have fun, get good jobs, find suitable romantic partners, and at the same time be pious Muslims, while Sarah Tobin (2016) examines how Jordanian Muslims reconcile their personal piety with matters of money and personal finance. By highlighting the diversity of religious views in Muslim societies as well as the complexity of their politics, the everyday Islam approach resists dominant representations of Muslims as abstract or inhuman entities. My work on the improvised and situational aspects of Islam, too, aims to foreground "our" shared humanity with Muslims and challenge the comfort that we take in "our" distance from "them" (which has made it easier for Western governments to drop their bombs on Muslim lands).

By focusing on religious improvisation and how it has produced unusual kinds of pious behavior, I want to make a case for the importance of allowing ourselves to be surprised by Islam. It is the same sense of astonishment that Michael Gilsenan ([1982] 2005) sought to foster in his classic study of how Islamic practices are bound up with many dimensions of social life in ways that are unexpected. "My own experience of Islam," he writes at the beginning of the book, "began with a surprised and uncomfortable recognition that things are not what they seem." Surprise is important to knowledge; it can be, as Jane Guyer (2013) points out, "an instigator to thought." Surprise can help to demystify dominant approaches to the religion and its followers in media and politics today. In particular, it is the unflinching assurance with which Islam is frequently treated in popular discourses, as an entity that we know to be this or that way, that ought to be disrupted. We should be able, for example, to read about Muslims who step on broken glass as part of their religious socialization, the ethnographic description with which I began this book, and not automatically assume that it has something to do with terror or radicalism.

Let me describe a major element of surprise in contemporary Indonesian Islam. Early in my fieldwork, I discovered that university campuses had become fierce battlegrounds for ideological factions seeking influence over undergraduates. I observed one such contest (in 2009) at the Syarif Hidayatullah State Islamic University, the flagship campus of state Islamic universities. The mood in the university at that time was distinctively somber. A few weeks earlier, a deadly bomb explosion occurred at the J. W. Marriott Hotel in Jakarta's commercial district. Police investigations identified the culprit as Jemaah Islamiyah, the radical group responsible for bombings in Bali in 2002 and 2005 and an earlier attack at the same beleaguered Marriott hotel in 2003. A more perplexing discovery was the involvement of a couple of male students from the State Islamic University with Jemaah Islamiyah. This finding shocked many Indonesians who assumed that terrorism attracted only the uneducated and the marginalized and not the learned youths. Many students at the university expressed great sorrow that their religion continued to be plagued by acts of violence legitimized by a particular interpretation of scripture. "Every time a fool detonates a bomb," wrote a student on his personal blog, "the collective insistence of a billion Muslims that Islam is a religion of peace becomes meaningless."

Participants from Formaci, the liberal Muslim student organization based at the university, decided to organize a seminar discussing the relationship between Islam and terrorism. Titled "The Global War against Terrorism" and held at one of the biggest lecture halls at the university, the seminar featured three speakers who were well known in Indonesia. The first was a North American woman who was an expert on security issues in Southeast Asia. The remaining two were Indonesian men: an anthropologist and professor of Islamic studies at a university in Yogyakarta, and a religious leader and leading proponent of liberal Islam who was pursuing a graduate degree in an American Ivy League institution following a lifelong stint in Islamic educational institutions. Each presentation touched on similar themes of terror networks in Indonesia and around the globe, the socialization of terrorists, and the responses of the state and citizens toward terrorism. The audience was politely receptive to the security expert, whose talk focused on the sociology of terror groups. The subsequent presentations by the professor and the religious leader, however, stirred up controversy. Both were extremely critical of orthodox Islamic theology, arguing that there are authoritative theological texts permitting Muslims to carry out acts of terror. Both insisted on the importance for Muslims to reevaluate their reading of religious texts, given the proliferation of jihadi-style attacks in recent years.

During the question-and-answer session, a young woman of about twenty came to the microphone that had been set up at the center aisle of the lecture hall. Dressed in a long-sleeved Arab-style dress and a head scarf that revealed only her face but covered everything else from the waist up, this young woman introduced herself as an undergraduate from the University of Indonesia, the country's most prestigious secular university. She was also a member of the Campus Proselytization Association, the Islamist student organization. She said that her questions were for the professor and the religious leader. In the beginning, she addressed the speakers with a firm but measured voice. "Both of you are painting a negative picture of the Quran and Muslims by associating Islam with terrorism. None of you mentioned the injustices that have been brought upon Muslims worldwide. You are merely perpetuating stereotypes about Muslims that have been created by the global media. And who controls the global media? Capitalists! Westerners! Jews!" By now her voice had reached a crescendo, its volume further amplified by the microphone. She then unleashed a barrage of questions that sounded more like accusations. "How could you side with them? Don't you feel guilty? Are you people even Muslims?" The people seated near me, mostly students from the State Islamic University, began hooting and whistling in delight at the unfolding spectacle.

Tapping into his microphone, the religious leader asked for the audience to be quiet before he rebuked the young woman. "It's unfortunate that students from our country's best educational institution, the University of Indonesia, are subscribing to such stupid ideas on Islam," he said sternly. "Students and professors here at the State Islamic University may look up to the University of Indonesia in fields like medicine, science, and engineering. But Islam is the domain of the Islamic university. You must defer to us in matters of religious opinion." Still standing at the aisle of the lecture hall, the young lady looked to be at the brink of tears as she was handed the public scolding. Meanwhile, the audience applauded the religious leader's remarks thunderously and laughed heartily at the one who dared to challenge him, though I did see some people approaching her after the event and commending her for her bravery.

Despite the obvious religious differences between them, the religious leader and the young woman shared a quality that reflected the improvisational ethos of the post-Suharto period. In both individuals, there appears to be a mismatch or an incongruence between their respective educational background and politics: the religious leader (a liberal Muslim) was educated in the Islamic educational system, while the young woman (an Islamist) was from the secular educational system. Their educational backgrounds represent the ideal typical characteristics of Islamists and liberal Muslims. Islamists, who advocate for the implementation of sharia law, tend to study secular subjects like medicine, science, and engineering, while possessing little formal education in religion. This is why Islamist organizations like the Campus Proselytization Association find the greatest success in secular universities like the University of Indonesia. In contrast, liberal Muslims, who are defenders of religious freedom and pluralism, tend to spend their early educational years in religious seminaries—which are generally known as madrasas, but which Indonesians distinguish between Islamic day schools (Indonesians call these *madrasa*) and Islamic boarding schools (*pesantren*)—and go on to study subjects like Islamic theology, Islamic philosophy, and Islamic jurisprudence at the undergraduate level.[12] Consequently, liberal student organizations like Formaci find the most support in the various branches of the State Islamic University.

Like the many Western academic audiences to whom I have presented my work, I was initially surprised by these findings. An analysis of Suharto's rule and the aftermath of its collapse, as I will provide later, can explain why Islamists and liberal Muslims emerged from particular educational institutions. But why might these educational institutions and the religious ideologies they produced seem so paradoxical? It is paradoxical only if we assume certain things about religion. As Talal Asad points out, religious knowledge is often regarded by Western liberals as traditional (in the sense of being concerned with preserving status quo and obeying figures of authority), irrational, and as expressing subjective belief rather than the objective truth (1993). This perspective hinders us from conceiving of people steeped in religious knowledge, like the liberal Muslims, as capable of advocating for values that are regarded to be progressive. The problem is further compounded by the negative reputation acquired by the madrasa in recent decades. Madrasas have been popularly regarded as jihad factories since the Taliban assumed control over Kabul in 1996 and especially after the 9/11 attacks. In response, scholars of Islam have argued that madrasas teaching radical ideologies are not only an isolated minority, but also cultivated by American and Pakistani intelligence as part of a Cold War strategy to wrest control of Afghanistan from the Soviet Union.[13]

Western liberalism also assumes certain things about secular knowledge. In contrast to religious knowledge, secular knowledge is regarded as unconstrained by authority figures or personal passions. It is seen as objectively committed to assessing the truth of arguments. Arguments must enter the marketplace of ideas, where rational debate decides which among them is superior. If we regard these assumptions to be true, then it is difficult to conceive that a secular educated person can become an Islamist who defends illiberal values. Prevailing beliefs that secular knowledge is rationally superior to religious knowledge are perhaps also informed by the notion that religious beliefs are simply more rigid than secular convictions. However, there is no decisive evidence supporting such claims. Religious traditions have in fact repeatedly proven their flexibility by undergoing radical transformations over time, as evidenced by the new methods of cultivating piety proposed by the Indonesian Islamists and liberal Muslims. "Divine texts may be unalterable," as Asad says, "but the ingenuities of human interpretation are endless" (1993, 236).

Prevailing assumptions about religion and Western liberalism prevent us from appreciating how they can intermingle. This was evident in many popular Western commentaries on the 2015 terrorist attack at the office of *Charlie Hebdo* that resulted in the deaths of several cartoonists. Many commentators interpreted the Muslim condemnation of the magazine's publication of the Muhammad cartoons as a sweeping rejection of values like freedom of speech and democratic citizenship. These commentators were unable to conceive that Muslims can be influenced by religious and secular ideals at once—or that they are capable of rejecting the satirical depictions of their prophet *and at the same time* rejecting the murders of the cartoonists. In cases where the confluence between religious and secular knowledge is acknowledged, the result is assumed to be some kind of psychological defect. In analyses of radical groups like al-Qaeda, for example, many Western commentators regarded their mixing of tradition (the desire to implement sharia law and establish the global Islamic caliphate) and modernity (the use of modern weaponry and media technologies) to be the main cause of their pathology, which is why these groups are often psychoanalyzed. Rather than an abnormality, however, religious and secular knowledge always intersect with one another, and it is this encounter that lies at the heart of the imaginative enterprise of both Islamists and liberals in contemporary Indonesia.

Plan of the Book

The story that I am telling unfolds over the next six chapters. Chapter 1 describes the student organizations where I conducted my fieldwork and the data collection methods I used and introduces some key interlocutors like Rizal and Hassan. Dominant historical narratives portray youths like them as key agents of Indonesian nationalism, which is why young people in Indonesia have long been permitted to feel a sense of tremblingness, or that quivering, can't-hold-back, impatient desire to change their society and nation. This enduring youthful capacity for tremblingness, I suggest, propels contemporary acts of religious improvisation. At the same time, as chapter 2 will elaborate, the ability of my interlocutors to religiously innovate was also enabled by the fall of the New Order in 1998. Unlike life during authoritarianism, democracy meant that religious identity is no longer subject to the same degree of microscopic governmental surveillance. People are able to try on different religious identities as they join various ideological groups at once, or move between them, and pursue different strategies to deal with the enlargement of secular liberal ideals in this context. The flurry of religious improvisation produces the counterintuitive patterns of Islamists emerging from secular schools and liberal Muslims from madrasas.

Chapters 3 and 4 are a pair. They examine how Islamists and liberal Muslims, respectively, translate between Islam and the secular liberal ideals that have become dominant under democracy. Guided by different religious interpretations and different interests in liberalism, these rival Muslim believers develop different types of improvised practices. Islamists want to groom ultraorthodox believers who are punctilious about ritual performances—persons seemingly different from the secular liberal subject. Yet Islamists make use of accounting and auditing technologies from the business world because they find them useful for creating the self-governing believer. Although Islamists have at times rejected democracy, there are democratic impulses in their religious improvisation. By forming devout and auditable subjects, Islamists hope to lay the foundation for the creation of a transparent, corruption-free, and pious nation before God. Liberal Muslims, on the other hand, want to inject values like individual autonomy, gender equality, and human rights into Islam, and do so by reading the Islamic scriptures through the lens of Western human sciences. These activities occur in private study settings that permit insults, jokes, laughter, and play, which render religious doctrines vulnerable and thus ultimately changeable.

The focus of chapter 5 is how the acts of religious improvisation intersect with political attempts to present Indonesia internationally as a "moderate" Muslim nation that is different from the "despotic" and "chaotic" Middle East. Although Muslims of different ideological stripes are actually capitulating to the West and absorbing the ideals of secular liberalism, the moderate Muslim discourse identifies liberal Muslims as "good" believers while denouncing Islamists as "bad" believers in need of liberal salvation. Blaming violence and discrimination on "bad" religion, however, promotes the view of religion as bounded and coherent and overlooks the complex constellation of factors that produce social ills. I reflect on this lesson and others in the epilogue, where I make the case for what Indonesia's improvisational Muslims can teach us about making a habitable coexistence in today's world.

1

THE TREMBLINGNESS OF YOUTHS

Protests are a ubiquitous feature of student life in Indonesia, but the ones
that are considered to be so brazen are talked about long after the events
have concluded. When I began my research in 2008, I heard numerous re-
tellings of a protest in 2004 involving a group of liberal Muslim students
who publicly accused their university administrators of religious misin-
terpretation. The confrontation took place at the State Islamic University
in Jakarta, a campus that was then in the midst of a corporate rebranding. In its pre-reform years, the campus was known as the State Institute
for Islamic Studies and offered instruction only in Islamic theology and
doctrine, with the mandate of producing new generations of religious bureaucrats. From 2002, as it refashioned itself from a religious institute
to a full-fledged university offering a broad-based education, the campus began to open new secular faculties and a graduate school. The university was presented to the nation as its crown jewel of higher Islamic
learning, a showcase of Islamic modernity where it was possible to teach
religious and secular subjects under one roof. But the university's public

image convinced administrators that Islamic symbols should play a prominent role in campus culture. In 2004, they introduced a new policy making it compulsory for female undergraduates to wear the head scarf when
on campus.

"It was a terrible, sexist decision," recounted Rizal, who had participated in protests against the policy. "How can you tell women what to
wear? And if she doesn't dress that way, does that mean she'll be de-
prived of an education?" He thought that the policy was incongruous
with the burgeoning awareness of women's rights issues since Indonesia's
democratic transition in 1998. In 2000, for example, the government issued the Presidential Instruction 9/2000 on Gender Mainstreaming directing all state agencies at the national and local levels to implement
gender equality in their policies and activities. Alongside governmental
initiatives, there was also a mushrooming of nongovernmental organizations advocating for the protection of women's rights and the prevention
of violence against women. Feminist themes were centrally discussed in
the novels by female authors like Ayu Utami and Intan Paramaditha and
the films of directors like Nia Dinata and Ucu Agustin. Male advocates
of feminist causes were also proliferating, most prominently the religious
leader K. H. Husein Muhammad. These newly emerging discourses circulated widely among Muslim progressives like Rizal and his friends in Formaci, the liberal Muslim study circle based at the State Islamic University.
A mixed-gender but mostly male group, Formaci's participants thought of
themselves as feminist allies and decided to protest the head scarf policy.

The protest occurred almost haphazardly. Rizal recalled much discussion among his friends about the head scarf policy that did not lead to the
making of concrete plans. "Then one morning, when I was still sleeping,
someone came into my room and said wake up, wake up, we're protesting
today," he said. A quick shower later and off to campus he went. About
twenty people from the reading circle had gathered in front of the rector's
office. A hastily prepared pamphlet titled "Jilbab Yes, Tak Berjilbab Yes"
(Head scarf yes, no head scarf yes), which argued for social acceptance
for whatever women chose to wear, was distributed to the undergraduate crowd that had gathered to see the protest.[1] Several participants from
Formaci took turns giving speeches. A young woman spoke about how
Islam has always conceptualized the head scarf as the private right of
the individual (*hak privat*) that cannot be forced upon someone by other

individuals or a corporate body. The next speaker, a young man, stated that the head scarf policy was counterproductive to the university's aspirations to become a cosmopolitan place of Islamic learning, as it would deter women, especially non-Muslims, from applying. These speeches were met with grumblings from the participants of conservative Islamist student organizations who supported the head scarf policy. Another young man from Formaci, irritated by the crowd's response, channeled his anger into his speech. "The administrators who planned this policy are religious fundamentalists," he hollered. "If this policy represents the true face of Islam, if this is a religion that forces people to do things against their will, then today I declare myself to be out of Islam!"

As he listened to his friend's spontaneous, heat-of-the-moment pronouncements, Rizal immediately came to the panicked realization that there would be a fierce backlash. Apostasy is not something Muslims treat lightly; in some authoritative scholarly traditions, it is punishable by death. True to Rizal's predictions, on that day and in the days to come, Formaci's participants were heckled by conservative Islamist students, who assaulted them with not only words but also with fists on three separate occasions. In the classrooms, they were rebuked by their professors. When the incident was reported in the local papers, members of Formaci began to receive anonymous threats over the phone. One caller said that because they insulted Islam, their blood becomes halal, which would make their murders religiously permissible. Fortunately, no attempts were made on the protesters' lives. But they were sorely disappointed that the protest did not change the administrators' minds on the head scarf policy. The policy was soon implemented, making the head scarf compulsory for female undergraduates while on campus grounds.

The protest, involving Muslim students who drew on liberal concepts of freedom, exemplifies the kind of religious improvisation possible in Indonesia since the fall of the New Order. Improvisation, as I have argued earlier, is a central feature of all religious life in the sense that religious believers constantly adapt religious scriptures and doctrines, through trial and error, to the vernacular and the vicissitudes of time. Religious improvisation is most acutely observable during "hot cultural moments—at the edges of life, in times of social upheaval, confusion, or transition, when old orders give way and what is ahead remains unclear" (Orsi 2003, 173). Moments of social dislocation, such as Indonesia's shift from authoritarianism to democracy, allow people to mobilize religious rhetoric to stake out certain positions for themselves in the changing landscape of power.

But just what summons these Indonesian student activists into action? Why did Rizal and his friends believe that they have a right to publicly rebuke their college administrators for their religious interpretation? Why did the conservative Islamist students feel that they should defend the head scarf policy and make threats on the liberals for their religious pronouncements?

Like the students involved in the protest, Indonesian youths generally regard themselves as legitimate participants in important public conversations. This sense of entitlement is not new. In his classic analysis of the 1945–1949 anticolonial war that secured Indonesian independence from the Dutch, Benedict Anderson (1972) observes that the youths living in that turbulent context were experiencing *kegelisahan*, a word whose literal meaning is "uneasiness" or "agitation" but which he brilliantly translated as "tremblingness."[2] These youths were seized by the nascent nationalist sentiment in their society, perhaps even more strongly than the older generation, in part because they were the first generation of Indonesians to receive a formal education and to develop their yearning for political independence through schools.[3] Tremblingness led these youths to pick up arms, join paramilitary groups, and launch the war for independence. Youths in post–New Order Indonesia, including Rizal and his friends, are also driven by a kind of palpitating impatience for change. They deploy religious arguments in creative ways because they sense that the moment is ripe for spiritual and political reform. Like the youths who have come before them, they act because they feel morally responsible for their society and nation.

Fieldwork among Student Activists

Although Indonesia is the world's most populous Muslim nation (nearly nine-tenths of its 250 million citizens profess Islam as a religion), it has been somewhat overlooked in the field of Islamic studies.[4] This is largely because of Indonesia's geographical and cultural distance from Islam's putative center, the Middle East, and perhaps compounded by how systematically Suharto tried to suppress Islam during his rule and promote secular nationalism and Javanese mysticism as the guiding frameworks for everyday lives. Yet Indonesia offers exciting opportunities for the study of religion and politics in a globalized world. Over the past few decades, Indonesia has gone through a dramatic political reform, as well as an Islamic religious reawakening and an expansion of the Muslim middle class. Mosques have been built at an accelerated pace; people began flocking to religious study circles held in homes and mosques; the Islamic fashion industry boomed as young women became more conscientious about head coverings than their mothers were; businesses started sending their employees to Islamic self-help programs; savings for the pilgrimage to Mecca were channeled to Islamic banks; and Islamic-themed shows appeared on television and at cinemas with regularity. Muslim political groups also began posing more abstract questions about Islam's relationship to the nation-state and offering different possibilities. Desires for consumerism, social transformation, and political power are enfolded in contemporary Indonesian Islam, thus giving shape to the kinds of religious improvisation I describe in this book.

Based in Indonesia's capital city, Jakarta, my research sought to understand how university students were dialectically shaping and shaped by the developments in religion and politics in Indonesia. University students are a tiny minority in this developing nation. According to official statistics, the proportion of the population who have tertiary education hovers around 3 percent.[5] While the seemingly low tuition fees should make university education more accessible—for example, a student in Islamic thought and philosophy at the State Islamic University pays 1 million rupiah per semester (approximately US$100 in 2008), while a student in the social sciences and humanities at the University of Indonesia pays about 5 million rupiah per semester—these costs are prohibitive in a nation where the per capita gross national income is only slightly above US$3,000.[6] Despite their small numbers, great symbolic importance is placed on university students. Popular narratives frequently celebrate university students as the midwife of Indonesian democracy, with the takeover of the House of Representatives by thousands of student protesters in 1998 identified as the pivotal moment when Suharto conceded defeat. As I began my fieldwork, I wondered about the impact that students have on the democratic era they helped to create.

Indonesia's dual educational system meant that I had to compare student activism in secular and Islamic universities (which are administered by the Ministry of Education and the Ministry of Religious Affairs respectively). Although students can switch between systems at any point in their educational career, most of the students I knew remained in one system from elementary school to university. The secular university where I conducted my research is the University of Indonesia (Universitas Indonesia). It is regarded as the best national institution for higher education, consistently sitting atop local university rankings, and is often Indonesia's sole representative in Asia-wide rankings. It is also the oldest tertiary-level institution in the nation, formed out of the small vocational colleges established from the mid-1800s by the Dutch for purposes of training native doctors, engineers, and lawyers. More than forty-five thousand students are enrolled in twelve undergraduate faculties (medicine, dentistry, nursing, public health, mathematics and natural sciences, engineering, computer science, law, economics, cultural studies, psychology, and social and political sciences), as well as in the graduate school.

My research at Islamic universities focused on the Syarif Hidayatullah State Islamic University (Universitas Islam Negeri Syarif Hidayatullah). It is the flagship campus of the nationwide Islamic university system, which traces its roots to a small college established in the 1940s to produce new members of the religious bureaucracy. The university has approximately twenty-five thousand students in six Islamic faculties (pedagogical sciences, ethics and humanities, Islamic thought and philosophy, law, proselytization and communication, and Islamic theology). In a modernization push in recent years, a graduate school and five secular faculties were established (psychology, economy and business, science and technology, medicine and health sciences, and social and political sciences), though students in secular faculties must take compulsory courses on Islam. While the State Islamic University may not have the prestige that the University of Indonesia enjoys, members of the religiously educated elite regard the Islamic university as the best of its kind in Indonesia as well as Southeast Asia more broadly.

At both universities, I discovered many organizations students could join if they are interested in activism. These included student government, campus presses, advocacy groups for social justice, groups based on religious and political affiliations, and reading circles. Each group usually has a small number of core participants and a sizable number of transient or occasional participants. There is, therefore, fluidity in the identity of an activist, since a politically active student can cease all organizational involvement to focus on studies (Indonesians call such students "SO," or study oriented), just as a politically apathetic student (known as *hedon* or hedonist) can become committed to the student movement when galvanized by certain issues. Activist organizations can either be official student bodies recognized by the university (*intra kampus*), which means that they receive funding from the campus administration and can use campus facilities for their events, or groups that are not officially recognized (*extra kampus*) and that do not enjoy the same privileges but are also less constrained by the rules put in place by the administration. As an indication of how adept activists are at circumventing regulations, these two types of groups often collaborate to maximize their relative advantages.

Among the multitude of activist organizations at the University of Indonesia and the State Islamic University, I spent most of my time with just two. The ideological persuasions of these two organizations seemed paradoxical, given their institutional locations (though paradoxical only if we accept conventional wisdom on religion and secularism). First is the Islamist organization called the Campus Proselytization Association, which was based at the University of Indonesia and attracts a largely secular-educated membership. The second is the liberal Muslim group Formaci, based at the State Islamic University and hence comprising mainly madrasa-trained participants. These groups have different organizational structures. The Campus Proselytization Association has *intra kampus* status, is larger (with almost two hundred regulars, compared to fewer than fifty for Formaci), and is part of a national network of Islamist student organizations. Formaci, on the other hand, is *extra kampus* and has no formal affiliations to other student bodies. However, these differences are not as sociologically significant as the one commonality binding them. Both the Campus Proselytization Association and Formaci are stairways to elite political status, as their former participants have become among the leading Islamist and liberal Muslim politicians, civil society activists, and public intellectuals in contemporary Indonesia. In other words, these two student groups are preeminent locations for the reproduction of Islamist and liberal Muslim ideologies in the nation.

The primary activity in both organizations is learning. Muslims regard learning as incumbent to piety, which is why, "in any Islamic society," as Michael Lambek observes, "everyone is engaged to some degree in the never-ending tasks of learning, reproducing, and passing on the sacred texts" (1993, 11) and why pedagogy is arguably the dominant focus in the anthropology of Islam.[7] With both groups, I participated in periodic meetings (held between one and three times per week) where students read and teach one another the texts that are regarded as foundational to their respective core values. Learning occurs in mixed-gender settings in Formaci, whereas the Campus Proselytization Association enforces gender segregation. I was not permitted to attend female-only activities in the Islamist organization, but hired a female research assistant to be a chaperone for interviews with female participants. Beyond the reading circles, I joined in other student activities, such as administrative meetings, street demonstrations, film screenings, and election campaigns. I also hung out with the student activists at homes, bookstores, mosques, cafés, and malls in order to observe their daily lives. Depending on the activity, I would either audio record the interactions or take copious notes by hand and type out more detailed ones each night. Bahasa Indonesia (the official language of Indonesia) was my primary medium of communication with the activists, with the occasional code-mixing with English and Arabic.

As I am an American-trained researcher who planned to spend time with rival Muslim organizations, I was initially afraid that the student activists would accuse me of being a spy and prohibit my research. My fears turned out to be unfounded, as I enjoyed relatively easy access to the student organizations. The access was made possible by several important politicians, civil society activists, and religious leaders whom I had gotten to know through my academic contacts in Indonesia. These members of the political and religious elite were former participants of the Campus Proselytization Association and Formaci and were addressed as "seniors" by my interlocutors. Given how these seniors unlocked the doors to my field sites, I immediately recognized the imbalances of power between them and the students, which is why the senior–student dynamic became a central motif of my research. I examined how the political elites cultivated student support for their political projects. I also analyzed the supplementary contributions that the seniors made to the students' autodidactic learning—for example, when they provide didactic instructions on how to understand a particular ideological text or when they define what constitutes a good performance in student activism through the incentives they disburse.

I had originally assumed that I would feel a sense of camaraderie with liberal Muslims, given that I self-identify as a progressive. My interlocutors quickly disabused me of these assumptions. Differences in nationality and age, among other things, meant that the liberal Muslim students never saw me as one of their own. For example, in a very common way of ascertaining the degree of foreignness from tropical Indonesia, they kept asking whether it was cold in my country of origin, Singapore (answer: no, it's always hot and humid there). People also often said that as someone who grew up in a developed nation, I could never understand the problems faced by developing nations like Indonesia. The alterity that I experienced turned out to be beneficial for my research, as it reminded me that my enterprise was analytical and not normative or autobiographical. Politically progressive researchers, especially if they are from Muslim backgrounds, tend to portray liberal Muslims as "good" or "moderate" Muslims who possess the correct interpretation of Islam. Such claims are intended to counter dominant representations linking Islam to violence and intolerance. However, the celebration of liberal Muslims misses out on the fact that whether something is Islamic or not is determined not by researchers but by debates among Muslims. It also overlooks how categories like "good" or "moderate" Muslims are not discursively neutral, but emerged in attempts to determine which Muslims can be aligned with Western projects of empire.[8]

Although disagreements with my conservative Islamist interlocutors lasted the entire duration of my fieldwork (especially over their views on non-Muslims, religious minorities, and gender and sexual minorities), I never saw them as "culturally repugnant others" (Harding 2000). Given that winning critics over was central to their mission, the Islamist students consistently and patiently engaged me in dialogue instead of simply chastising or alienating me for my views. My fieldwork also enabled me to observe cultural practices that were recognizable and that rendered the Islamists less strange. As an academic, I appreciated that my young interlocutors took their education very seriously and strove hard to attain good grades. As someone who has struggled in the job market, I applauded their tenacity in trying to get good jobs. As a believer in democracy, I admired the Islamist commitment to upholding transparency, anticorruption, and accountability in Indonesia. Yet Islamists approached these activities differently from the way I would, given that they regarded the performances of the activities as essential to their piety. Nevertheless, the fact that Islamists cannot escape these activities underscores the common humanity between them and everyone else who must contend with the hegemony of capitalism, democracy, and Western liberalism in today's world. Even if we do not like Islamists, beginning from an empathetic stance allows us to better understand the effects of global forces and why Islamists respond the way they do. Empathy and criticism, after all, do not have to be zero sum options.[9]

Youths and the Nation

Hassan, the Islamist student who was an accounting major at the University of Indonesia, was one of my most important informants on Indonesian student activism. His journey to student activism was fairly conventional. When he moved to Jakarta from his hometown in Padang to attend college, he thought that joining a student organization was a good way to make friends. An acquaintance from high school was a member of the Campus Proselytization Association and urged him to join as well. The organization quickly became a "total social fact" (Mauss [1923] 2000) in Hassan's life as it began to structure his daily routine. He took the same accounting classes as his friends from the organization and attended tutoring sessions conducted by more senior activists. He exercised regularly with the same people, playing soccer on some days and badminton on others. He began to hatch entrepreneurial plans with a few of these friends, which, depending on the day I talked to them, ranged from setting up an Internet café to selling bedsheets and hijab fashions, though they eventually decided to explore the refurbished cell phone business. The interactions between Hassan and other students recall the point consistently made by scholars of religion that people join religious fraternities for complex motives that are often not reducible to a pietistic quest.

Like many of his friends, Hassan lived in a "*kost* house" located about a five-minute motorcycle ride away from campus. The *kost* (from the outdated Dutch expression *in de kost*, meaning to live in a guesthouse) is a dormitory-like building with bedrooms for rent and shared facilities like kitchens, living rooms, and Muslim prayer rooms. Typically located close to university campuses and commercial districts in Jakarta, the *kost* is the standard accommodation for students, young professionals, and migrant workers who do not own property or live in their family homes. Rents vary according to levels of comfort. A "high end" *kost*, which comes with air-conditioning, en suite bathroom, and laundry and housekeeping services, costs at least 3 million rupiah per month (approximately US$300). Hassan, however, opted for a cheaper room priced at US$50, which he shared with one friend from the organization. *Kost* houses are often the source of hand-wringing among Indonesians who believe that living independently of parental supervision permits youths to engage in undesirable conduct, particularly of the sexual kind, which is why many *kost* are single sex and forbid guests during overnight curfew hours. Yet there is another type of freedom that the *kost* provides, one that complements the autodidactic setting of the reading circles, which is that it offers its inhabitants the privacy to engage in religiously and politically improvisational behavior.

If there was something that he thought would help my research, Hassan would make it a point to describe or show it to me. One day, he invited me to his *kost* to show me a poster he had put up on the wall. The poster is popular among student activists. It depicts a young man with bloodshot eyes and an agape mouth that appears to be roaring, as he seems determined to break free from the chains shackled to his hands. The only pop of color in the otherwise black-and-white poster is provided by the red of the red-and-white Indonesian flag unfurled behind the young man. At the bottom of the poster is the caption "Boeng, Ajo Boeng!" (Lads! Come on, lads!). Inspired by the come-hither calls of prostitutes seeking customers, the caption attempts to seduce its audience toward a different type of pleasure, the pleasure of nationalism. Designed in 1945 by the Indonesian artist Affandi Kusuma, the poster was propaganda commissioned by the nationalist leader Sukarno (who eventually became the first president of Indonesia). It began circulating following the defeat of the Japanese in World War II (Japan had occupied Indonesia for three years during the war) and the ensuing attempts by the Dutch and their British allies to wrest Indonesia back to colonial status. In this unstable context, youths were called upon to take up arms in the struggle to secure the liberation of the nation.

According to Hassan, the poster had tremendous significance to student activists because it reminded them of their "obligations toward society" (*tanggung jawab terhadap masyarakat*). Indeed, established historical narratives describe youths as the stalwarts of Indonesian nationalism. Nationalism appeared in colonial Indonesia at the turn of the twentieth century. Taking advantage of a relatively benign period of Dutch rule, Indonesians formed voluntary organizations that were concerned primarily with cultural and educational objectives.[10] Although these organizations did not develop a clear political philosophy, their existence meant that there was a public sphere in colonial Indonesia, analogous to the eighteenth-century salons in Europe famously described by Jürgen Habermas (1962) where people could congregate and talk politics. Youths were important participants in these proto-nationalist Indonesian organizations. They were the first generation of Indonesians to undergo mass schooling, where they were exposed to the highly uniform scholastic practices such as similar textbooks and a strictly regulated separation of age groups. Such educational practices, in addition to the ability to read publications in the vernacular, created a coherent universe of experience for youths across the colony and led them to agitate for change. In this context, "the younger generation" (*kaum muda*) became a metaphor for social transformation.[11]

Hassan's poster, designed and circulated during the war for independence (1945–1949), marked the beginning of the politicization of youthful tremblingness in republican Indonesia. Ordinary youths mobilized in paramilitary groups and engaged in bloody warfare against their foreign rulers, a touchstone moment that gave moral permission for youth masses to participate in the reconfiguration of their nation.[12] When Sukarno became Indonesia's first president (1949–1965), he implemented the annual celebration of Youth Pledge Day (Hari Sumpah Pemuda) on October 28 to commemorate the youth conference in 1928 where youths swore allegiance to nationalism. Youth vigor became a constant referent in Sukarno's nation-building projects, while separatists challenging Indonesian sovereignty were accused of "deviating from the oath of 1928" (Foulcher 2000, 388–89). In contrast, the subsequent administration of President Suharto (1965–1998) attempted to depoliticize youths altogether. Suharto, an army general, staged a coup against the leftist Sukarno regime

and unleashed a campaign of extraordinary violence against people regarded as Communists or Communist sympathizers. Approximately half
a million or more suspected Communists were killed, not only by soldiers,
but also by young civilian executioners from street gangs, militias, and Islamic seminaries. Having attained power with the help of youths, Suharto
eventually became threatened by their tremblingness and implemented a
series of policies to restrain them, including the ban on student activism
in 1978.

Student activists in post–New Order Indonesia, regardless of their political or ideological affiliations, are taught about the chronicle of important
events involving youths in the nation. It was during one such history lesson, conducted by the Campus Proselytization Association, that Hassan received the poster he showed me. During these lessons, the past generations
of youths are referred to by the years of their politicization. The "Generation of '45" (*generasi '45*) referred to those who fought for Indonesian
independence; the "Generation of '66" stemmed the Communist influence
in the nation, the "Generation of '78" were the first to experience the ban
on activism, and the "Generation of '98" set the nation on the path of
democratic reforms (see also Steedly 2013a). The history lessons on the
preceding generations of student activists are, however, not simply about
the past, as student activists would then be asked to reflect on the possible
contributions that they can make to their society. It is a type of memory
practice that Daniel Rosenberg and Susan Harding (2005) call a "history
of the future," which is when people attempt to imagine their future by
referencing how historical subjects imagined their own futures. In such
exercises, student activists will have to examine if they possess the same
commitment that their predecessors showed, and indeed, whether they can
tremble like them.

Islam and the Nation

When considering the various ways they can contribute to the uplift of
their nation, my interlocutors often employed Islamic vocabularies. Islam
for them was not simply a matter of private faith, but also an ideal vehicle
for the advancement of public life. Hassan, who was a member of the outreach and publicity committee of the Campus Proselytization Association,

had been involved in creating a video meant to encourage commitment to student activism. "We wanted to make something emotional because students don't show up when they get too busy with other things," he explained as we watched the video on his laptop. Messianic in its tone, the video was certainly over the top. Visually, it was essentially a slide presentation of the various street demonstrations in which the students of the organization had participated, interspersed with journalistic images of poverty in Indonesia. The sequence of the slides went something like this: activists, homeless children, activists, crippled panhandlers, activists, mothers foraging for food in the trash, and so on. These images were accompanied by orchestral music dominated by an uplifting melody on the trumpet and the bold beat of percussion. The following text scrolled across the screen one line at a time:

Prepare yourselves!!!	Persiapkan diri antum!!!
To welcome victory	Untuk menyambut kemenangan
O fighters	Wahai para pejuang
For Allah's promise is certainly true	Bahwa janji Allah pasti benar
And victory is only a matter of time	Dan kemenangan itu hanya masalah waktu
Your contributions, hard work and prayers will hasten its arrival	Kontribusi, kerja keras dan doa akan mempercepat kedatangannya
Should we remain quiet!!!	Apakah kita hanya bisa diam!!!
When our nation's sovereignty is robbed	Ketika negara kita dirampok kedaulatannya
No!!!	Tidak!!!
O youths	Wahai para pemuda
The suffering of this nation is your responsibility	Derita negara ini adalah tanggungjawab kalian
Work, work, and work on	Bekerja, bekerja, dan bekerjalah
God is great!	Allahu akbar!

Several days later, with the sense of tremblingness in the video still fresh in my memory, I followed my interlocutors in the liberal Muslim organization Formaci to an activist training program bringing together a network of liberal Muslim students from universities across Indonesia. Abrupt transitions between time spent with Islamists and liberals were normal in my fieldwork. Instead of being disruptive, however, the constant back-and-forth movement enabled me to better appreciate the continuities and discontinuities between the two groups. The three-day liberal Muslim training program I attended was organized by a well-known civil society organization called the Lembaga Studi Agama dan Filsafat (Institute for the Study of Religion and Philosophy) and held in a rented bungalow in the mountain resort town of Bogor, a popular weekend destination for Jakarta city dwellers. The program consisted of talks and discussions led by seniors in the liberal Islam movement that were structured around a manual produced by the organizers. In the preface of the manual, the organizers made a case for the urgency of creating new generations of liberal Muslims. Describing post–New Order Indonesia as a "democracy without civil liberties" (*demokrasi tanpa kebebasan sipil*), the organizers blamed the Islamists for promoting religious intolerance in the nation. The organizers argued,

Therefore, we face the critical and urgent task of building and strengthening a network of young Muslims who are able, on the one hand, to provide a critical response toward narrow-minded Islamic discourses and paradigms, and on the other, propose solutions to the practice of Islam in a modern, plural Indonesian context. More specifically, this generation of Muslim youths that we aim to groom are those with the means and desire to champion the principles of freedom and pluralism in the practice of religion in Indonesia. Additionally, these Muslim youths should realize that the principles of freedom and pluralism in religious practice can be accomplished only when the principles of secularism, liberalism, and pluralism are upheld.

Oleh karena itu, dirasa sangat perlu dan mendesak untuk membangun dan memperkuat jaringan generasi muda Muslim yang mampu berfikir kritis terhadap wacana dan paradigma keislaman yang exclusif pada satu sisi, dan mampu menjawab persoalan-persoalan keislaman dalam konteks kemoderenan dan keindonesiaan di lain sisi. Secara khusus, jaringan generasi muda Muslim dimaksud adalah mereka yang mau dan mampu memperjuangkan prinsip-prinsip kebebasan dan pluralisme dalam kehidupan beragama di Indonesia. Lebih jauh lagi, mereka adalah generasi muda Muslim yang menyadari bahwa prinsip-prinsip kebebasan dan pluralisme dalam kehidupan beragama ini hanya bisa dicapai dengan memperjuangkan diskursus sekularisme, liberalisme dan pluralisme.

A comparison of this text with the Islamist video reveals interesting parallels between the two rivals in terms of their references to nationalism. This similarity may not be immediately apparent, given the divergences in their politics. Islamists believe that systemic problems in Indonesia like poverty are caused by the secular government's neglect of piety and therefore locate the solution in the submission to God's commandments; liberals, on the other hand, believe that Islamists worsen problems in Indonesia and thus advocate for an Islam compatible with liberal values. In spite of these dissimilarities, however, the respective projects of these two groups aim to improve the nation. Islamists want to recover "the nation's sovereignty," while liberals want to create "plural Indonesia." Of these two rivals, it is the nationalism of the Islamists that may be surprising to some readers. Particularly since the rise of transnational radical groups like al-Qaeda and, more recently, ISIS, there are widespread assumptions that Islamists are committed to the creation of the global Islamic caliphate. Yet, as Charles Kurzman (2011) argues, such assumptions overlook the variations among Islamist groups in terms of the polities they want to create. The Taliban, for example, had nationalist ambitions over Afghanistan and did not share the global aspirations of its close cousin al-Qaeda. The appeal of nationalism to conservative Islamists should therefore not be underestimated.

In their respective attempts to define Islam's place in Indonesian politics, Islamists and liberals are participating in a contentious debate that has been waged since at least the turn of the twentieth century.[13] The fundamental disagreement between them—whether Islam should have a privileged role in the nation or not—is not new. The nationalist leader Sukarno, worrying that Muslims would demand the formation of an Islamic state, published an essay titled "Nationalism, Islam and Marxism" ([1927] 1970) to urge for Indonesian unity under the banner of secular nationalism.[14] Sukarno's struggles with Muslim privilege were palpable in the Pancasila, Indonesia's official political ideology that he crafted together with other founding fathers during the time of independence. Aiming to include different cultures, ethnicities, and religions in the membership of Indonesia, the Pancasila consists of five principles: (1) belief in a singular God; (2) a just and civilized humanity; (3) the unity of Indonesia; (4) democracy; and (5) social justice. The first principle gives official recognition to five major religions in Indonesia (Islam, Protestantism, Catholicism, Buddhism, and Hinduism) by conceptualizing them as monotheistic religions.[15] This principle was initially opposed by Muslim leaders for not explicitly privileging Islam. To accommodate them, Sukarno amended the wording so that it read "belief in a singular God with the obligation for adherents of Islam to practice Islamic law."[16] When secularist leaders expressed reservations about the potential coercion this new formulation could cause, Sukarno reverted to the original wording.

The Pancasila has consistently remained at the center of state and non-state attempts to define proper Muslim subjectivity in Indonesia. To subdue his political opponents, Suharto defined the Pancasila as the best guide for Indonesian society, as it embodied "age-old" and "indigenous" principles and was thus superior to "foreign" ideologies like Islam or Marxism. His New Order government implemented an indoctrination program called P4, where everyone from primary school children to civil servants had to attend courses and take exams on the Pancasila.[17] In the democratic era, the Pancasila became a source of contention among the religious and political factions fighting for influence. Revisiting Sukarno's dilemma from decades past, conservative Islamists proposed that the first principle of the Pancasila should be amended to the version that gives special dispensation for Islam (that included the phrase "with the obligation for adherents of Islam to practice Islamic law"). Opponents of the Islamists, however, vehemently argued that the Pancasila is binding, which means that there is no room for the formal implementation of sharia law. As a result of the public backlash, Islamist politicians subsequently backtracked and professed their fealty to the Pancasila.[18]

The unceasing debates about religion's place in Indonesia offer important insight into the workings of secularism. Hussein Ali Agrama (2012) usefully conceptualizes secularism as a "questioning power" in the sense that it continually questions and renders vulnerable the very norms that it creates. Secularism draws boundaries between religion and politics and erases them at the same time, hence creating ambiguity. In the case of Indonesia, the secular Pancasila ideology simultaneously makes politics the objective of religion as it attempts to turn religion into an object of politics. The key heritage that Indonesia's founding fathers have left behind through their formulation of secularism, therefore, is one where there is a space for disputations over religion and politics to rage on continuously in the nation, with uncertain outcomes.[19] Indonesia, from this perspective, is an "unfinished nation" (see Lane 2008). Through their respective projects of religious improvisation, both conservative Islamist and liberal Muslim youths are attempting to chart a more certain future for the nation, not only by asking how the line between religion and politics ought to be drawn, but also by asking how to improve people's access to fundamental rights and liberties.

The Student and the Senior

While certain historical legacies permit Indonesian youths to participate in important national conversations on religion and politics, the awareness that they can play these public roles has to be implanted in them. Virtually all my interlocutors told an origin story on how they became an activist. The liberal Muslim student Rizal was no exception. Rizal dates his political awakening to the early 1990s, when he was a ten-year-old living in a small town in Sulawesi. During the day, he attended a secular elementary school; at night, he went to the neighborhood mosque to learn how to recite the Quran, the most fundamental skill in an Islamic education. The recitation class was taught by Mustafa, a recent graduate of Islamic philosophy from the State Islamic University. Mustafa left an indelible impact on the young Rizal, who regarded him as the teacher among teachers, the one from whom he acquired the most valuable knowledge. Mustafa not only taught his young charge about the holy scripture, but also conducted additional classes at no cost on an array of subjects from the Arabic language to science and philosophy. When Rizal was twelve years old, two years after he started learning with Mustafa, he had already acquired familiarity with the theories of Charles Darwin and associated debates pitting evolutionism versus creationism, something he did not learn in his elementary school.

In the following year, when Rizal was thirteen and about to enter middle school, Mustafa announced that he would be moving away. Mustafa had been a student activist when he was an undergraduate and wanted to continue making a difference in society. Some time later, Rizal received news that Mustafa had joined a nongovernmental organization that traveled to remote villages in Sulawesi's mountainous regions to establish primary schools. Mustafa and his colleagues would stay at each village for several months to build the school and conduct training for the villagers designated as teachers, before journeying on to the next village that needed a school. Rizal was so moved by what his teacher was doing that he decided to emulate him. The first act of imitation was in terms of education. Rizal switched from the secular to Islamic educational system and eventually enrolled in the State Islamic University to major in Islamic philosophy. The second act of imitation was in terms of activism. At university, Rizal decided to devote his time to social causes and joined various activist organizations including the liberal Muslim group Formaci. I noted that as he was telling me his origin story, Rizal consistently referred to Mustafa as his "senior."

Seniors, as I have stated previously, loom large in student activism. Older in age from a few years to a few decades, the senior can be a friend, a roommate, a teacher, a cousin, or an acquaintance from the same hometown. The senior has experience with activism and ignites the student's interest in social causes. The senior can lead students to activism unintentionally, as in the example of Mustafa's influence on Rizal, or in most cases deliberately, by simply inviting students to join particular organizations. Students typically develop close relationships with seniors of their same gender, though cross-gender mentorships occur as well. Regardless of the age gap between them, the relationship between a student and the senior is akin to the relationship with an older sibling rather than a parent. The senior is therefore addressed as either "older brother" or "older sister," using terminologies specific to the senior's ethnic background, such as *kang* or *teh* (if the senior is Sundanese), *bang* or *kakak* (Malay), or *mas* or *mbak* (Javanese). The senior is never addressed as *bapak* (father) or *ibu* (mother), which are terms of address reserved for people who are more distant in the social hierarchy.

Seniors fulfill important pedagogical functions. They give practical advice on managing student life, for example, what the best university courses are, or where to find cheap accommodations. They also impart particular religious and political ideologies by designing the syllabi used by student reading circles and providing guidance on textual interpretation. While often supportive and encouraging, seniors do not shy away from criticizing their juniors. Hassan, the conservative Islamist student, introduced me to his thirty-something-year-old senior named Achmad, who had participated in the massive demonstrations that toppled Suharto. The stories Achmad told me were stuff of adventure novels and action movies. He described how seemingly everyone in 1998 was seized by antigovernment sentiments. He talked about the fateful day at Trisakti University, the congregation point for protesters before marching to the House of Representatives, when he witnessed four student activists shot by military snipers. He knew the student leaders who hid in different *kost* houses each day because they were being pursued by the army. My impression of Achmad was that he told these stories not only to bask in nostalgia but also to discipline his juniors, as he frequently complained that the younger generation were lazy (*malas*), hedonistic (*hedon*), and study oriented (SO). Supposedly more interested in self than society, they have disappointingly failed to live up to the standards set by their predecessors.

Such criticisms of their tremblingness often motivate students to spring into action. In 2009, a group of University of Indonesia undergraduates invited me to an event that was named "Back to Campus." The event was organized by the Himpunan Mahasiswa Islam (Assembly of Muslim Students), which was one of the oldest and largest undergraduate associations in Indonesia but whose popularity has plummeted with the rise of newer groups like the conservative Islamists and the liberal Muslims in the post–New Order years. With the aim of reversing the decline in membership and reestablishing the organization's prominence on campus, the event featured an exhibition of photographs depicting activist glories from past years and a series of motivational talks by current and former members. There were also presentations on the new projects undertaken by the organization, for example the basic voter-education programs that aimed to teach residents who live near campus about free and fair elections. When I asked the student activists about the impetus behind the event, they said that they wanted to assure their concerned seniors that the organization was not falling into political irrelevance. In other words, through the use of positive and negative motivation, the seniors ensure the continual transmission of nationalistic fervor.

Why people dedicate themselves to nationalistic projects is a topic of extensive scholarly debate. Portraying the nation as a quasi-religious entity that provides answers to existential questions, Benedict Anderson (1983) suggests that people are willing to die for their country because sacrificing one's individual mortality for the collective immortality of the nation is a compelling idea. Other scholars argue, however, that people's participation in nationalist projects is not inevitable. In his study of Greece, Michael Herzfeld (2005) discovers that the patriotism of ordinary people can be driven by the nation's mortality rather than its immortality—he observes, for example, that people support the nation-state when its corruption allows them to take advantage of class inequalities and enjoy the comforts of everyday life. Likewise, in her study of the marginalized Karo people who fought for Indonesian independence, Mary Steedly argues that the routes people take to nationalist projects are often divergent, as are the stories people tell about the subject: "Gender is written into the scripts of nationhood, in voices that speak of patriotism as well as violence, sacrifice as well as opportunity, 'tiredness' as much as bravery; in the intimate, familiar language of home as well as the aspirational rhetoric of the transcendent nation-state" (2013a, 17). Both Herzfeld and Steedly tell us that nationalism must be understood through an analysis of practice and agency rather than through a teleological lens.

Among the most important elements of practice and agency in Indonesian student activism are the rewards that seniors can distribute to the students who show commitment and promise. Particularly prized are the jobs at the various institutions that are run by the seniors. Rizal, for instance, was offered a full-time position at a liberal Muslim nongovernmental organization when he graduated from the State Islamic University. The director who hired him was impressed by Rizal's devotion to social causes, since he spent so much time volunteering and interning at various civil society groups while he was still an undergraduate (which, as I mentioned earlier, distracted him so much from his studies that he took a full decade to complete his bachelor's degree).[20] Similar to other cultural contexts, student activism can offer an opportunity for Indonesian youths from lower-working-class or petit bourgeois backgrounds to climb the social ladder and become part of the nation's political elite.[21] This is not to suggest that Indonesian students have solely calculative or instrumental motives for participating in activism, though they are, like their counterparts elsewhere, justifiably worried about job prospects in a tightening neoliberal economy. Rather, this is to point out, as Karl Marx ([1867] 1992) reminded us so long ago, that the material cannot be separated from the ideological.

Recruiting student activists into the various institutions administered by the seniors is essential for the reproduction of the political class. Once he got his job, Rizal was invited to a conference in Manila aimed at building a network of Muslim progressives in Southeast Asia (the conference was organized by Malaysian liberals in 2010 with funding from a German philanthropic association; I attended as a delegate from Singapore). Though initially excited to travel outside Indonesia for the first time, Rizal became daunted by the experience. He spoke English haltingly and struggled to keep up with the conference proceedings. Consequently, the forty-something-year-old senior who invited him there, a veteran of transnational travel and meetings, had to intervene each time Rizal could not articulate his views cogently. The senior told me that he hoped Rizal and other young activists will quickly gain confidence so that he did not have to attend similar events in the future. Having spent many years on the conference circuit, the senior was eager to embrace the new challenge of becoming a public intellectual on matters pertaining to religion and politics. "My editor is already chasing me for my book," he explained as he pounded away furiously on his laptop at the back of the room, participating only halfheartedly in the conference discussions.

The senior, in short, is like the student's guide through time and space. Like a master to an apprentice (see Herzfeld 2004), seniors link the student activists to the future by grooming them and eventually allowing them to take their place, so that the religious and political movements to which they belong can live on. They also connect the student activists to the past. It is through their seniors that the students become aware of the structural conditions permitting youthful displays of tremblingness and meaningful engagement with pressing religious and political concerns in society. By sketching out the history and sociology of student activism in this chapter, I have therefore sought to establish that religious and political improvisation, or spontaneous forms of behavior that draw on whatever resources may be available, are integral to the experience of Indonesian youths. In the following chapter, I examine the particular forms of improvisation that are possible in Indonesia's age of democracy. Specifically, I am interested in the encounter between Islam and liberalism, and the assemblages produced by the trial-and-error attempts to mediate the encounter. To examine these and other issues, we must now turn to the upheavals that occurred when Suharto was suddenly and spectacularly removed from power.

2

RELIGION UNLEASHED

Surveillance of religion by President Suharto's New Order government meant that only certain religious types were permitted during Indonesia's authoritarian years. For the New Order, a regime that rose to power amid the throes of the Cold War by slaughtering masses of suspected Communists and overthrowing a left-leaning incumbent government, proper management of religion was crucial to political order. Religion was prescribed as the antidote to atheism, which was widely perceived as a synonym for communism.[1] The government encouraged people to embrace religion, whether by means of religious learning, worship, or consumption, but with the condition that such expressions of religiosity be kept within their private lives. While the government regarded private piety favorably, it was threatened by public religion, or more specifically, the political ambition offered by religion. Islam, the religion of most Indonesians, was especially problematic because it offered the Islamic state and the global Islamic caliphate as political alternatives to the secular nationalism of the New Order. To curtail such ambitions, the regime routinely kidnapped and tortured dissenting religious leaders and coerced Muslim organizations to plead allegiance to Pancasila, the state nationalist ideology, rather than to Islam.

Following the democratic transition, Indonesia sought to cut the legacy of the New Order through political and economic decentralization, a process that Indonesians call *pemekaran* (meaning "blossoming" or "flowering"). New administrative and budgetary units were formed in the provinces with the aims of reducing the power of the Jakarta-based central government, increasing local participation in politics and economics, and enhancing ordinary people's sense of belonging to the nation. These political and economic reforms also encouraged a cultural renaissance as people began producing and consuming art, literature, and films to make sense of the upheavals in their society. Religion, too, became unleashed in this context. New religious types appeared, proposing new ways of being Muslim that transcended the limits that the New Order previously imposed on religious practice and imagination. However, as the new religious types had different ideas about Islam's place in the nation, they also engaged in fierce contests with one another to dictate the terms of public discourse. Protests and counterprotests between religious factions were so widespread during the post–New Order period that I must have attended an average of one street demonstration per fortnight during fieldwork.

In 2008, for example, I observed rival protests staged by two new religious factions. The object of contestation was the Antipornography Bill. As noted by Webb Keane (2009), the expansion of the freedoms of speech and press resulting from Indonesia's democratic transition raised concerns regarding the limits of such freedoms. In the House of Representatives, Islamist legislators from the Prosperous Justice Party proposed a new bill to safeguard public morality by outlawing the production and dissemination of pornographic materials. The Antipornography Bill offers a good insight into the evolution of the political strategies employed by the Islamist party. During the 1999 elections, shortly after its founding, the party made strident calls for the establishment of the Islamic state and Islamic law. When these proposals were rejected by the majority of Indonesian voters, the party downplayed its initial demands and instead emphasized the compatibility between Islam and democracy. The conciliatory tone with regard to democracy led to greater success in subsequent elections, enabling the Islamists to become one of the biggest factions in the House of Representatives.[2] Islamists used the legislative platform to push for new secular laws (like the Antipornography Bill) that are informed by a foundational aspect of Islamic doctrine, which is "to enjoin what is good and forbid what is evil."[3] In other words, this was sharia via the democratic process.

As the House of Representatives discussed whether or not to pass the Antipornography Bill, parallel disputations took place in the national media, on university campuses, and in the streets. At nine in the morning on October 23, 2008, about three hundred Islamist student activists from various secular universities in Jakarta gathered outside the main gates of the compound of the House of Representatives to show their support for the Antipornography Bill. It was a lively scene. A male student leader gave a speech using a megaphone on how the law would help to eradicate vice in Indonesia. Male and female undergraduates waved placards with catchy slogans like "Say No to Porno" or "Tolak Porno" (Reject pornography), handed out informational pamphlets to the motorists who slowed down or pulled over to watch the demonstration, and gave interviews to reporters, who had been contacted several days earlier. A large contingent of police officers monitored the gathering, while street vendors peddled beverages, snacks, cigarettes, and counterfeit designer sunglasses. Curiously, I noticed that one of the student leaders I knew seemed to be more fixated on his cell phone than the hubbub that surrounded him. He told me that he was exchanging text messages with his seniors—the Islamist legislators in the House of Representatives—who wanted live updates on the demonstration.

By noon, the Islamist students boarded the buses chartered to take them back to their campuses, and a different group of students then assembled at the House of Representatives. They picked the same date as the earlier group not because of coincidence but because the legislators were expected to vote on the proposed law later that day (though the vote was eventually postponed for a week). Police allocated different time slots for these groups to prevent skirmishes. There were about two hundred people in this second group, which consisted of liberal Muslim students from Islamic universities, as well as their seniors from various nongovernmental organizations and arts communities. They took issue with how "pornography" was defined in the Antipornography Bill—namely, as any pictures, photographs, animation, films, music, speech, embodied movement, sculptures, and other forms of media that aroused sexual desire and/or offended prevailing cultural norms. In the pamphlets they distributed, the protesters highlighted three concerns. First, given Indonesia's cultural diversity, whose cultural norms would be used to determine that moral injury has occurred? Second, could seduction really be ascertained by legal means? Third, given prevailing cultural ideas that view women as seducers, would the law be used to restrict women's behavior (for example, the clothes they wear and the jobs they perform)? Liberal Muslims were thus concerned that the law served Islamist interests at the cost of freedom and pluralism in the nation.

Questioning the boundaries between sexual proprieties and improprieties was a recurrent theme in the speeches made by several activists. From the back of a pickup truck that served as a makeshift stage, a male activist addressed how the law could lead to further discrimination against Indonesia's indigenous communities should their traditional costumes like loincloths and penis sheaths be regarded as sexually enticing and hence pornographic. After him was a young woman who spoke coquettishly as part of her performance. "I like muscular men and men in uniform. And I am very aroused by the police officers here. Does this mean that the police officers are pornography? Should they be banned?" The crowd chuckled at her speech, as did a number of police officers. A few minutes before three in the afternoon, when the demonstration was scheduled to end, a young man tried to lead the crowd in a cheer. "Reject the Antipornography Law now!" he howled. "The law is porno!" (*undang-undangnya porno*; the word "porno" could mean lewd, obscene, or immoral in this context). "Those who proposed the law are porno! Those who supported the law are even more porno!" Beside him, two other young men dressed in curly wigs, lipstick, and women's clothing danced in an exaggerated feminine manner. The exhilaration of protest for these liberals, however, turned into disappointment about a week later when Islamist legislators managed to get enough support in the House of Representatives for the Antipornography Law to be passed.

The contests over the Antipornography Law reveal one of Islam's most important features. Debates and disputations, as numerous scholars have argued, are fundamental to Islam. In their work on the Quran, Michael Fischer and Mehdi Abedi (1990) challenge the commonly held view that Islam is prescriptive. They describe the Quran as a profoundly enigmatic text whose meanings lie beyond human capacity for definitive exegesis. To understand the Quran, Muslims rely on other sources like the hadith (sayings of the Prophet), the *sunna* (the precedents of the Prophet) and the historical contexts of the revelations—which themselves require authentication and interpretation. The work of scriptural interpretation is thus like a "fun house of mirrors" (116) that is open-ended and necessarily dialogic. Likewise, Muhammad Khalid Masud, Brinkley Messick, and David Powers (1996) describe Islamic law as not something that is simply imposed top-down in draconian fashion, as it is often portrayed in popular media. Rather, the law develops through dialogue and collaboration between religious scholars and lay Muslims. It is by answering religious questions posed by lay Muslims that scholars devise legal rulings and keep Islamic law up-to-date with continually evolving historical contexts. Scholars have also shown that religious debates are not the exclusive purview of religious elites, as ordinary Muslims, like the villagers in remote Pakistan in Magnus Marsden's study (2005), also partake in them.

However, dominant representations of Islam since the beginning of the "War on Terror" tend to overlook the important role of internal debates. Interest in security has resulted in a singular fixation on the conservative Islamists who are opposed to liberal values. Commentators on Islam have devoted plentiful attention to the socialization of youths in conservative Islamist groups, debated strategies of keeping youths away from such groups, and celebrated the redemptive stories of ex-Islamists who somehow managed to turn away from the errors of their ways.[4] Other Muslims are either invisible or at best helpless. It has seemed inevitable that each time an extremist kills in the name of Islam, a chorus of voices in the Western public will express anger, frustration, or even incomprehension as to why "moderate" Muslims have remained silent (Ibrahim 2015). Silence, however, is not an attribute of Muslim societies. Rather, the crowded political landscape of the post–New Order period, where a multitude of actors and ideologies are competing with one another for hegemony and influence, offers a more accurate, if heightened, representation of Muslim societies. Cacophony, therefore, needs to be re-centered in contemporary analyses of Islam.

To understand the possibilities of religious and political life in the post–New Order context, it is useful to turn to Anna Tsing's work (2005) on an Indonesian resource frontier, the rain forests of South Kalimantan where timber is procured by legal and illegal entrepreneurs for distant markets. Tsing observes that these capitalists do not simply carry out their activities freely and without constraints. Instead, they encounter environmental movements that arose to defend the rain forests, as well as a wide range of other global and local actors for whom the rain forests were important, from North American investors and UN funding agencies to village elders, mountaineers, the army, and nature-loving urban students. Tsing develops "friction" as a metaphor for the diverse social interactions between the many actors in the frontier zone. Friction leads to uncertain outcomes: sometimes it produces conflict and misunderstanding between the actors, at other times, convergences. Speaking against the image of global capitalism as a triumphant, well-oiled machine that swallows up local societies, Tsing calls attention to the importance of friction—and the struggles, debates, and conversations it brings—in the continual reproduction of capitalism.

The religious and political world of the post–New Order era resembles the interstitial capitalist zone described by Tsing. There are conservative Islamists, liberal Muslims, and a whole host of other religious factions, state and non-state actors, women and men, and students and their seniors, all hoping to make their mark in society. Tsing tells us that the interactions between the many actors in a social universe produce outcomes that cannot be determined in advance. Foregone conclusions, therefore, should be treated as suspect. For example, although they are widely regarded as the most illiberal and antiliberal among Muslims, the conservative Islamists who live in Indonesia's democratic age engage with liberal values in ways that are not simply tantamount to rejection. Conservative Islamist politicians introduce policies like the Antipornography Bill only after they have been democratically elected to the legislature. Furthermore, at its core, the Antipornography Bill poses a question about whether limits should be placed on freedom of speech, an issue that is endlessly debated in Western societies. Following the student activists as they navigate the contested religious and political landscape of democratic Indonesia, this chapter describes the emergence of Muslim beliefs and practices that are improvisational and in defiance of convention and expectations.

DIY

Imagine you are an undergraduate in Jakarta in the post-Suharto era. You are likely to be living away from your parents for the first time in your life, either because your family home is not in Jakarta, or, if it is Jakarta, you rent a *kost* near campus to avoid commuting in the city's notorious traffic jams. When you step on campus during freshman orientation week, perhaps to register for classes or make purchases at the bookstore, you will inevitably be accosted by recruiters from various student organizations, much the same way that arriving passengers at an airport are swarmed by taxi drivers offering a ride to the city. Most recruiters will be from Islamic organizations, which are typically some of the largest groups at the university. As the recruiters offer to take you on a campus tour or navigate the labyrinth that is the university bureaucracy, they will also invite you to a recruitment event at their organization. You think to yourself, "I could make some new friends," or "I'd like to learn about religion," as you decide to accept the invitation. Since you received similar invitations from several organizations, you might check out all of them to determine which you like best, even if their religious orientations are opposed to one another. When you have multiple personal objectives to fulfill and multiple religious groups clamoring for your attention, your religious identity is not static but likely made up as you go along.

DIY or "do it yourself" religion is the term that Elizabeth Hurd (2015, 127) gives to such practices that do not necessarily follow conventional or recommended religious scripts written by religious authorities. DIY religion can be taken as a synonym for the improvised religious forms that are rapidly blossoming in the post–New Order era. This political context has also witnessed the proliferation of DIY cultural practices among youths beyond the sphere of religion, particularly in the creative industries. Brent Luvaas (2012) examines the "indie" music and fashion scene in Indonesia, which is populated with youths who are fueled by a neoliberal entrepreneurial ethos and working with no more than cheap digital technologies. Taking cultural production into their own hands, they start their own fashion lines and record labels. Luvaas argues that by tearing down the barriers between production and consumption, these young indie entrepreneurs are helping to create a collectivist alternative to global capitalism that is not simply imposed top-down but emerging from the ground up. In other words, their DIY cultural practices have broad and significant repercussions, the same way the improvised practices of young Muslim believers also help shape the terms of public debate on religion and politics.

I learned a lot about religiosity in a crowded religious world from Nuriya, a young woman at the State Islamic University whom I hired to assist me with interviewing female student activists. We met when Nuriya was in her final year of college and had just completed a senior thesis on the Islamist movement in Indonesia. Once, she asked me if she would make an appearance in my book, and when I said yes, she promptly decided that her pseudonym would be Nuriya. "It's what I wished my parents had named me," she said. She was feisty and strong-willed, which you might not have guessed from her appearance, as she was only five feet tall and always clad in modest Muslim attire, typically a loose long-sleeved blouse, long skirt, and a billowing head scarf that reached below her waist. Actually, it was her rebelliousness that got her into university in the first place, as she had to go against parents who did not think women should be too highly educated. Nuriya grew up in a Central Java village that was a world away from the Jakarta metropolis, a place so remote that no cell phone reception could be detected. In this farming community, young women were typically married off soon after completing high school. "It's better to be a young widow than an old maid," was a local saying that spoke to the cultural distaste for delayed matrimony.

Coming of age in a post–New Order era where feminist ideals began to circulate widely, Nuriya conceived of alternative possibilities for her future. In her final year of high school at a local madrasa, she attended a seminar on women's empowerment organized by a Jakarta-based nongovernmental organization, where the keynote speaker, Madam Dorita, emphasized the importance of higher education for young women. Impressed by the speech, Nuriya approached Madam Dorita to request her name card but was too shy to ask more questions. When her parents brought up the issue of marriage following her high school graduation, Nuriya stated that it simply had to wait, because she wanted to go to university. "You are on your own with this," her disappointed parents responded. "We will not support this plan." Determined to proceed but with no clear strategy in mind, Nuriya packed a bag of clothes and brazenly embarked on the ten-hour bus journey to Jakarta, where an acquaintance agreed to put her up temporarily. The only other person she knew in the city was Madam Dorita, so she decided to go to her office. "Madam, I want to study, but I have no money," said Nuriya, pleading for a solution. Moved by the young lady's resolve, Madam Dorita found her a job at the liberal Muslim NGO where she worked (which was where Nuriya and I were first introduced) and helped her apply to the State Islamic University.

Once she was admitted to the university, Nuriya, along with other freshmen, was courted by the various student organizations on campus. Like many of her contemporaries, she joined multiple groups. The culture shock of moving from one group to the next, particularly with groups that are ideologically antithetical to one another, is mitigated by how student organizations generally conduct their activities in similarly formulaic fashion. A seminar, for example, often begins with a *kontrak belajar* (a learning contract), where participants will have to collectively agree on the values to which they will abide during the activity: for example, everyone must come punctually, everyone must speak up, all opinions will be respected, cell phones must be switched off, and so on. Intensive training programs are often held at rented villas in small towns on the outskirts of the Jakarta metropolis, typically at Puncak if students want to enjoy cool mountain weather, or at Anyer for a seaside environment. These shared cultural practices therefore facilitate the circulation of students between organizations, which in turn enabled me to conduct research with a variety of different groups without ever being asked to declare my "true" ideological or organizational sympathies.

Having checked out various student groups, Nuriya decided to become a member of the Islamist-oriented Campus Proselytization Association, a seemingly unusual choice for someone whose benefactor was a liberal Muslim feminist. Although indebted to Madam Dorita, Nuriya never felt comfortable identifying herself as liberal, given that she was raised in a religiously conservative household and was educated in a conservative madrasa. Seeking to replicate a similarly devout experience on campus, she joined the organization she judged to be the most concerned with piety. But the Islamist group soon disappointed her. Having assisted Madam Dorita on research projects regarding gender equality, Nuriya found it disconcerting that many Islamists supported polygyny, a practice that is permissible from the perspective of classical Islamic doctrine but widely regarded as undesirable by Indonesian Muslims. She was mortified that many of her female friends in the organization were being propositioned by men much older than they to become second wives. "Why don't you quit the group?" I asked, puzzled by her tentativeness in this regard. "I thought I could help reform the views of the group's participants," she rationalized. I discovered that there was much at stake for her personally. She had a romantic interest in a young man in the Campus Proselytization

Association who believed in a man's right to multiple wives and was hoping that he would change his mind. (I will have more to say about her romantic interest later.) Caught between her mentor and her crush, Nuriya thus found her loyalties split between two competing movements.

The kind of DIY religiosity exhibited by Nuriya has often been overlooked in analyses of Islam. For example, scholars who take the self-cultivation approach to the study of Islam, as I have discussed earlier, focus on how religiosity is attained through a rigid and continuous maintenance of ascetic discipline.[5] However, this model of consistent habituation represents only one example of Muslim religiosity and does not stand for all of Islam. A more capacious theorization of Muslim subjectivities should pay more attention to journeys like Nuriya's, where people experiment with various identities, make things up as they go along, do something unexpected, and change their minds. Nuriya's exploration of multiple ideological orientations, after all, is neither uncommon nor unique to the crowded landscape of democratic Indonesia. Religious lives are often messy and unstable, precisely because religion is tangled up with multiple domains in society and is utilized by people in their pursuit of both religious and nonreligious aims. As a result, religious believers often lead lives that are rife with contradictions, even though they may not necessarily be bothered by these inconsistencies (see also Schielke 2015). This is why someone like Nuriya can at once be liberal Muslim and Islamist, at once capitulating to her feminist mentor and the (possibly polyamorous) object of her affection.

Conversions

DIY religiosity is an example of how people sought to resolve the major crisis of identity caused by the Indonesian democratic transition. James Siegel (2006) examined people's quest to understand where they belonged in relation to others in this context, focusing on the outbreak of witchcraft accusations and killings that occurred in East Java around the time of the New Order's collapse.[6] During Suharto's rule, only certain types of identities were permitted and recognized by the government, as there was always a need for people to show that they had letters of identification, identity badges, and permits. Siegel suggests that continuous surveillance was reassuring to Indonesians, even if they were critical of the New Order, because recognition by the state meant that one was not part of those whom the state finds menacing (and hence killable). When the source of that recognition was removed from power, however, there was tremendous uncertainty about "correct" identity. One could be someone utterly different from anything or anyone that one knows—one could even be a menacing figure like the witch. By murdering the people accused of being witches, the villagers in Siegel's study were attempting to reassert social control in a time of uncertainty. Nevertheless, Siegel suggests that the identity disorientations need not only result in murder, because if they were "harnessed to more advanced political thinking . . . the release of imaginative possibilities could have been used for radical change" (161). In other words, without an authoritarian state defining who people could be, new identities tied to new visions of society could then emerge.

As people joined the conservative Islamist and liberal Islam movements, just two of the new social types promising a brighter future for Indonesia, I observed that they often described their experiences using the tropes of conversion. By conversion, I am not referring to the movement from one religious tradition to another—for example, from Buddhism to Islam. Instead, I am referring to the process that Clifford Geertz (1973) terms "internal conversion," or the change in how one interprets and practices the same religious tradition. I observed that my student activist interlocutors would describe the religious U-turns they have taken by saying, for example, "I was not at all religious back then, but now I feel really close to God," or "I used to be a religious hard-liner, but now I'm liberal." These conversion tropes are socially significant. In addition to revealing the DIY quality of religious lives in the democratic era, they also importantly show that the context has allowed certain discernible patterns of religious socialization to emerge. I will describe two such instances of conversion, one showing how someone comes to embrace a conservative Islamist point of view, the other the liberal Muslim perspective. I hope to show that both ideologies are not universally attractive, but that each appeals to particular audiences.

My first conversion story is about Erwin, an engineering student at the University of Indonesia and a participant in the Campus Proselytization Association. Erwin is an ethnic Minang who grew up in the western highlands of Sumatra. He characterized his religious upbringing as "normal" (*seperti biasa*), or fairly congruous with the religious experiences of ordinary Indonesian Muslims. He was educated in secular schools from an early age and was also enrolled in a Quran recitation class at the local mosque for several evenings each week. "I didn't study religion too deeply," he recounted. "We recited the Quran in the class, and maybe memorized some passages, but we weren't taught scriptural exegesis or Islamic history or anything sophisticated like that." "Were you a rebellious adolescent, or were you well behaved?" I asked. "Definitely well behaved," he said, adding that he was a consistently top performer in school, carried out his religious rituals punctiliously, and did not smoke. He avoided misconduct partly because he was afraid of his maternal uncle, a fierce man who was also the head of the village where he lived. In this community, maternal uncles play an important role in a child's upbringing, because Minang culture is matrilineal.

At nineteen, Erwin flew on an airplane for the first time in his life when he moved to Jakarta for college. He made the journey on his own, because the ticket prices were out of his family's reach, which appropriately foreshadowed the life of independence that soon beckoned him. In Jakarta, he had to learn to do things he had never done before, like paying bills and cleaning the house, which he found tedious and cumbersome; but he did appreciate living far from the strict supervision of his parents and particularly his uncle. Unlike his disciplined and well-behaved adolescent self, Erwin was now a free young man who lived in pursuit of fun. He smoked, drank alcohol, frequently patronized billiard bars, and "freely associated" (*bergaul bebas*) with women. As though he knew what I wanted to ask next, he immediately clarified that he went on a lot of dates but did not engage in "free sex," the phrase Indonesians use to describe casual sexual encounters. His hectic social life meant that he devoted minimal effort to his coursework, which predictably resulted in a subpar academic performance. Life proceeded along, to use Erwin's term, a "hedonistic" (*hedon*) path—until a particularly sticky situation forced him to do some critical self-reflection.

In the second year of college, Erwin became chair of the University of Indonesia's Minang Students Association, a social networking group for students from this ethnic community. One of the first events that he organized was a badminton game, followed by dinner. As the event came to a close, a participant requested that Erwin recite a supplication (*doa*) as a formal way of concluding, a fairly typical practice in Muslim social activities. Erwin panicked because he had never memorized any supplications when he was a child, nor had he bothered to seek religious knowledge as a young adult. A ruse was thus needed to shield from public view his inadequacies as a student leader and as a Muslim. He quickly decided that the best strategy would be to exercise his authority and delegate the task. "The chairperson shouldn't have to do everything around here," he said. "I want to see some teamwork. Someone else should recite the supplication." Erwin managed to save face when another participant volunteered to do it, but internally, he felt humiliated. He was a student at the nation's top university, yet he was incapable of the simple act of reciting a supplication. As Erving Goffman ([1959] 1990) reminds us, people will go to great lengths to avoid embarrassment in social interactions, which was why Erwin concluded that the only way to prevent similar incidents in the future was for him to learn more about Islam.

Erwin decided to join the Campus Proselytization Association because it claimed to be the most devout Muslim group. Since it was common for activists to live together, Erwin moved in with several male Islamist students a few months after joining the organization. At home, his housemates included him in their daily discussions on religion, reminded him to perform his prayers, pressured him to stop smoking, encouraged him to do well in class, and even helped him carry out his original intention by teaching him some supplications. But Erwin felt unhappy about sacrificing his personal freedom for the sake of religious observance. Apparently serendipity is an important theme in his life, because once again a random incident prodded him to think about his religious commitments. During a camping trip with the Minang students, Erwin contracted malaria and had to be hospitalized for a week. His housemates visited him daily and even raised funds to pay for his hospital bills. Their compassion and tenderness touched him. From that point onward, he told me, he began to think that the pleasure he used to derive from bars, billiards, and women was only fleeting and hence "false happiness" (*kebahagiaan semu*), whereas the kindness and humanity that could only spring from religion represented "genuine happiness" (*kebahagiaan riil*). He proceeded to convince himself that his new life was what he really wanted.

Like Erwin's account of how he became part of an Islamist organization, the story of another student I encountered, Farouk, also contains themes of internal conversion. Farouk was an undergraduate at the State Islamic University and a member of Formaci. I asked him to tell me about how he came to identify himself as a liberal Muslim. Farouk was born in Padang, a religiously conservative city in Sumatra that had recently implemented sharia laws requiring high school students to learn the Quran and government employees to contribute part of their salary to alms (*zakat*). His father, who worked as a civil servant in the provincial office of the Department of Religion and also lectured in a madrasa, was a conservative man who supported the city's formalization of Islamic laws. Farouk was educated in the madrasa where his father taught, so it was expected that in terms of the views he had about the world, the apple would not fall far from the tree. According to Farouk, "When I was a teenager, I was obsessed with the idea that the West is only interested in oppressing Muslims. I believed that globalization and modernity were tools for oppression and a continuation of the Crusades. I remember that I would refuse to watch television or listen to the radio or consume Western items, like wearing jeans or drinking Coca-Cola, because I thought that they would tarnish my faith."

Farouk's religious views began to change when he enrolled in the State Islamic University, where he majored in comparative religion. He took classes on the world's major religious traditions, which slowly opened him to the idea that the values Islam cherished were also very much present in other religions. A classmate also invited him to Formaci's reading circles, but he did not take well to the group in the beginning. "I really thought these people were deviants or apostates," he recalled. "They were saying these crazy things, like prayers weren't the only way to worship God, that prayers don't indicate if necessarily a person is a good Muslim, that social justice is a form of worship. And many of them don't even pray at all, as though they were staging a rebellion against religion." I asked Farouk how he came to accept the group. He said that over many heated discussions and debates, he gradually came to understand that the group was trying to foster what he called a "humanistic" approach to religion, where fostering harmonious relations among human beings is regarded to be of utmost importance. He contrasted this with a "God-centered" approach to religion, where human energies are devoted to pleasing God, and hence prayers, fasting, and other ritual acts are emphasized. The more time Farouk spent with the group, the more he found himself subscribing to their arguments on religious pluralism, inclusiveness, and tolerance.

"I've been enlightened [*tercerahkan*] since coming to university," Farouk said, notably using the term that is so foundational to secular modernity. But what did he think about his younger self and the religious views he held then? He described the adolescent Farouk using a well-known Indonesian idiom, a frog who lives under a coconut husk and knows nothing about the world outside (*katak dalam tempurung*)—in other words, an ignoramus. Smiling wryly, he said, "I was such a fundamentalist back then." Farouk hesitated when I asked whether he also thought of his father in these terms. After a pause, he concurred, saying that he regarded his father's beliefs as "not progressive" (*tidak progresif*). The split in religious views between father and son has made Farouk's visits to his family home in Padang very tense. Talking about the place of Islam in contemporary Indonesia made each of them upset with the other, with the father bemoaning how Jakarta has corrupted the son, and the son griping about the father's narrow-mindedness. In a more recent visit, however, Farouk decided that it might be best to avoid conflict with his father, which meant that they could have only anodyne conversations that steered completely clear of religion and politics.

Indonesia's democratic age, as the two stories of internal conversion suggest, has given rise to new and somewhat counterintuitive forms of religious identities. Conservative Islamists tend to be people from the secular educational system, like Erwin, whereas liberal Muslims tend to be those from the religious educational system, like Farouk. These are what Max Weber calls ideal types—analytical constructs that overlook subjective variations in order to showcase the essential features of a social phenomenon (Gerth and Mills 1946). Both patterns of religious socialization may seem surprising in light of powerful assumptions about the superiority of secular knowledge over religious knowledge, as I have discussed previously. Western secular liberals regard secular knowledge as objective, rational, and unconstrained by charismatic figures of authority. Religious knowledge, on the other hand, is assumed to be subjective, irrational, and concerned with upholding dogma. However, the backgrounds of conservative Islamists and liberal Muslims suggest that religion and secular liberalism are in fact knotted up with one another in complicated ways instead of opposing each other in reductive ways. As we will see shortly, these entanglements are caused by New Order policies on religion and the efforts by ordinary Muslims to recast the relationship between Islam and modernity.

Secular Islamists, Religious Liberals

A genocidal campaign against Communists, aided in part by powerful Muslim organizations in the country, brought the New Order into power in 1965. Once it was in power, the regime sought to accomplish a political balancing act, on the one hand to minimize opposition from Muslims over its secular rule, and on the other to encourage private piety among citizens to prevent attraction to communism. To accomplish these twin aims, education was identified as a site of intervention. The Indonesian educational system is separated into a secular stream administered by the Ministry of Education and a religious stream administered by the Ministry of Religious Affairs, the former to produce participants in the modern economy, the latter to groom religious scholars and bureaucrats. From the government's perspective, the two educational streams produced diametrically opposed religious subjects, the religiously lax and the religiously learned respectively. To attain political order, it thus needed to attain some sort of inversion and make religiously lax youths more pious (so that they would not become Communists) and religiously learned youths more modern (so that they would not oppose the secular government).

From the 1970s, the government made it compulsory for students in secular universities to take courses on religion covering basic theology and doctrine. This created a job market for instructors on religion, filled mainly by Indonesian graduates from Egyptian universities. Egypt, home to the one of the most venerable institutions for religious learning, the Al Azhar University, has long been a choice destination for Indonesians pursuing an advanced Islamic education. Despite its wariness of the religiously learned, the New Order unintentionally led to an increase in the number of Indonesians heading to Egypt when it blocked conservative Islamists from electoral politics.[7] Barred from formal politics, Islamist leaders decided to focus their energies on cultural politics instead, with an emphasis on religious proselytization (*dakwah*). Through their institutional home, the Indonesian Forum on Islamic Proselytization (Dewan

Dakwah Islamiyah Indonesia), Islamist leaders procured Middle Eastern financial sponsorship to send Indonesian students to Egypt to study with conservative Islamist teachers. These students were eventually hired as instructors of religion in Indonesia's secular universities. They also helped introduce Muslim Brotherhood literature to the secular-educated students, which is why the new generation of Islamists that appeared in the post–New Order period are influenced by Muslim Brotherhood ideology.[8]

Parallel curricular reforms took place in the Islamic educational system. The New Order sought to update traditional Islamic education to produce new generations of Muslims who would not be antagonistic to secular modernity and the secular state. In madrasas (which offered education up to high school), secular subjects began to be taught using the same textbooks as in secular schools. At the university level, a doctrinal and normative religious pedagogy was de-emphasized in favor of Western scholarly approaches to the study of Islam. With the assistance of Western educational institutions like Canada's McGill University, undergraduates in Indonesia's Islamic universities began to be exposed to courses like anthropology, philosophy, and comparative religion, as well as liberal social attitudes on issues like democratization, religious pluralism, and human rights. These reforms were orchestrated by powerful political actors like Mukti Ali (minister for religious affairs, 1971–1978) and Munawir Sjadzali (minister for religious affairs, 1983–1993), as well as top university administrators like Harun Nasution (rector, State Institute for Islamic Studies, 1973–1984), all of whom went from a traditional religious education to eventually pursue graduate degrees in the humanities and social sciences in Western universities.[9]

The educational reforms account for why Islamists and liberal Muslims tend to be educated at secular and Islamic institutions respectively. Islamist and liberal Muslim youths who live in the democratic age, as the subsequent chapters will describe in greater detail, have the freedom to behave in religiously and politically improvisational ways as they transgress the boundaries between the religious and the liberal and invent forms of religious practices that draw on both worlds. During the New Order, however, the political energies of young people were repressed. Student activism was outlawed by the government in 1978, preventing youths from participating in overtly visible political activities like street demonstrations. Instead, these youths began to form quasi-underground study circles that met in *kost* houses and campus mosques and prayer rooms. Influenced by the changes that the government made to the educational curriculum, the study circles in secular universities read literature written by key Muslim Brotherhood ideologues, while those in Islamic universities tackled the great texts of Western civilization. In the guise of cultivating private piety, a new political consciousness began to emerge in these study circles, which were embryos that eventually developed into student organizations like the Campus Proselytization Association and Formaci.

As a result of the educational reforms, different modes of engaging with the religious scriptures emerged among Islamists and liberal Muslims. Islamists are an embodiment of the "modernist" turn in Islam that began around the early twentieth century. As John Bowen explains (1993), modernists not only advocate for the ability of Muslims to pursue business, science, and secular education, but also believe that piety need not be mediated by religious scholars. It is important to note that religious scholars have historically interpreted the Islamic scriptures in such vastly different ways that they tend to accept that there may be more than one appropriate way of carrying out one's religious duties. However, in cases where modernists, such as the Islamists, have limited exposure to the religious sciences, they often resort to a literal interpretation of scripture without making adequate space for nuance or variation in religious understanding that are associated with religious scholars.[10] Liberal Muslims are also modernists, in the sense that they rely on Western human sciences to formulate an interpretation of the holy scriptures. Yet, as they have spent a lifetime in Islamic religious institutions, liberals are at the same time "traditionalists" who consult the work of past religious scholars. In other words, the liberal Muslim acceptance of diversity in religious practice should not be attributed to the Western human sciences alone, as it is also shaped by traditionalist Islamic doctrine.

Comparisons with other cultural contexts indicate that the Indonesian patterns of religious socialization are not unique to the nation. Carool Kersten (2011), for example, studies intellectuals from various postcolonial Muslim nations who combine their grounding in the Islamic heritage with the Western human sciences to engage in a double critique of both Muslim and Western discourses on Islam.[11] Such analyses debunk the pervasive representations of Islamic knowledge as uncritical, backward, or, worse, the foundation of jihadi ideologies.[12] It is true that radicals have emerged from madrasas, particularly in Pakistan and Afghanistan in the 1980s, but such schools were cultivated by U.S. intelligence as part of the Cold War realpolitik and do not necessarily reflect intrinsic properties of religious knowledge. Actually, a growing number of studies, such as the one conducted by Charles Kurzman (2011), suggest that violent and nonviolent Islamists tend to possess secular educational credentials.[13] In their fascinating research, Diego Gambetta and Steffen Hertog (2016) even offered a more specific observation—that violent Islamist extremists tend to be engineers.[14] The proliferation of these studies suggests that we ought to rethink our assumptions about secular and religious bodies of knowledge, particularly how the former is seen as morally and intellectually superior to the latter. Instead, we should turn to other approaches, such as examining the interactions between these bodies of knowledge and the assemblages that are produced, to attain more meaningful insights into our social condition.

"Strange" Behaviors

Interactions between diverse actors and ideas in a frontier zone, as Anna Tsing argues in her study of capitalism, often produce surprising outcomes that cannot be predicted. I documented improvised religious and political forms that emerged in the similarly interstitial context of the post–New Order, which meant that I was regularly encountering unusual things during fieldwork. And they never ceased to astound. One of the strangest cases I observed had to do with Angga, an accounting student at the University of Indonesia who was also a member of the Campus Proselytization Association. Money seemed to be a central preoccupation in Angga's life. He grew up in a poor family in Madura, an island in eastern Indonesia, and if he had to rely on his family's income, there was no way he could have gone to university, especially in Jakarta. Fortunately, by virtue of his strong academic achievements, he managed to win a scholarship from the Madurese provincial government. The scholarship generously covered his tuition fees but offered a paltry stipend, so Angga constantly tried to live frugally. When traveling between Madura and Jakarta, he preferred the cheaper but slower option of passenger ships instead of flying, the preferred mode of cross-archipelagic travel for many Indonesians these days. In Jakarta, he rented a room in a wooden *kost* house, which was far more modest than the standard brick-walled accommodations that other students choose.

Driven by his personal circumstances, Angga pursued the neoliberal strategy of turning to entrepreneurship. He learned about business not in the classrooms of the university but at the Islamist student organization, which promotes a modernist interpretation of Islam and believes that Islam and business are compatible, as seen by how the student organization incorporates self-help and accounting and auditing practices into its religious activities. Angga pursued numerous entrepreneurial gigs. One day, he took me to a multilevel marketing company selling health-related products, with the intention of making a sale from me and, more important, recruiting me as a salesperson from whom he could earn a commission. He was selling magnetic bracelets from Japan, which he claimed could cure not only minor ailments like headaches but also life-threatening diseases like cancer. To show how the magnetic forces worked, he slapped a bracelet onto my wrist and hung onto my shoulders like a child on monkey bars. "Doesn't it feel effortless when you're carrying me? That's because the magnetic field is giving you strength," he said. "Yes, it's easy to carry you, but that's because you're so skinny," I responded skeptically. Like virtually every potential customer he approached, I declined to purchase the bracelet. Finding a lack of success, Angga soon quit the gig.

It wasn't long before Angga found a new entrepreneurial venture, which I discovered quite by accident. I was hanging out with him in the living room of his *kost* house one afternoon when someone came by. He introduced himself as Budi, whom Angga acknowledged as his neighbor and senior. Budi, in his forties, had a wife and children in Sumatra whom he had left behind while he pursued a master's degree in economics at the University of Indonesia. The three of us chatted until it was almost sundown, when Budi invited me to stay for dinner. He handed some cash to Angga and told him to purchase food at the neighborhood market. "Hey, don't forget to also buy the stuff that we need for tomorrow," yelled Budi as Angga dashed out the door. "Yeah, okay!" Angga replied from a distance. Eventually Angga returned bearing steamed white rice, a large barbecued fish, stir-fried mixed vegetables, a crispy omelette, and some bananas. Budi set the bananas aside, explaining that we would not be eating them tonight. "Angga and I need the bananas for our business," said Budi. I was intrigued—what kind of enterprise could it be?

Budi and Angga were offering a traditional massage service that Indonesians call Mak Erot (Mother Erot). Named after the famous woman masseuse who supposedly invented the technique, the Mak Erot massage promises to increase men's virility but is widely regarded as a euphemism for penis enlargement. There is much fascination about Mak Erot in Indonesian popular culture, and several plays and movies—such as one titled *XL*—have been made about her life. Mak Erot massage parlors can still be found in some neighborhoods across Jakarta, though they are increasingly getting replaced by stalls selling (probably counterfeit) sexual enhancement pills like Viagra. Budi had been performing the Mak Erot massage in his hometown for years and decided to continue doing it in Jakarta to support himself through graduate school. Available for in-calls and out-calls, Budi worked mainly with middle-aged and elderly male clients who lived in the neighborhood. Angga was his business associate who was mainly in charge of maintaining the client database, scheduling appointments, receiving payments, and occasionally buying bananas. The bananas would be used by clients to indicate to Budi the genital size they wished to attain.

I was taken aback not because Angga was a penis enlargement entrepreneur, but because he was a self-identified conservative Islamist who chose that particular line of work. One evening, as we were having a meal at Grand Indonesia, one of Jakarta's glitziest malls built in the post-Suharto neoliberal era, Angga also appeared to show some discomfort with how he mixed religion and entrepreneurship. As Grand Indonesia had the best cinemas in the capital, it was the choice screening venue for many film festivals, including the Q! Film Festival, a showcase of gay- and lesbian-themed films from across the globe, which was being held when Angga and I met. The film festival is an example of the public visibility enjoyed by gays and lesbians after the fall of the New Order. But the rise in gay and lesbian activism has been met with attacks by right-wing Islamist groups—even though such assaults have been rare historically. Tom Boellstorff (2005) suggests that the previous lack of antihomosexual violence should not be read as an acceptance of homosexuality, but as a condition of "heterosexism" where the naturalness and superiority of heterosexuality was unchallenged. The greater public visibility of gays and lesbians in the post-authoritarian era, however, became construed as a challenge to heterosexuality and thus needed repelling through violence. To defend heterosexuality, heterosexism is transformed into homophobia.

"These people are corrupting society," said Angga as he pointed disapprovingly to a publicity poster of the Q! Film Festival and cited the Quranic verses pertaining to the prophet Lot ibn Haran.[15] Muslims have largely understood the story of Lot and the people of Sodom and Gomorrah as a prohibition on homosexuality, specifically male-on-male anal penetration. However, contemporary reformist thinkers, who argue that interpretations cannot be severed from context and that a literal reading of the sacred texts is erroneous, arrive at a different conclusion. These reformers aim to revise established doctrines that are at odds with values like justice, equality, and respect for the inherent dignity of human beings—values they argue are central to Islam. They examine other aspects of Lot's story beyond the same-sex acts (describing, for example, how the people of Sodom and Gomorrah also committed murder and robbery) and argue that the same-sex acts were not problematic per se, but rather because they involved aggression and subjugating others by force (in other words, rape). For the reformers, the verses on Lot should not be narrowly understood as prohibitions against sexual transgression but as containing guidance against the dangers of spiritual corruption and violence more broadly. As they employ an esoteric vocabulary and sophisticated forms of argumentation that combine the Islamic heritage and Western human sciences, these reformers find support only among the highest-educated believers (for more details see Kugle 2010 and Ibrahim 2016).

Like most ordinary believers, conservative Islamists usually react to such reinterpretations with confusion and condemnation. An important factor shaping the Islamist response is that Islamists tend to be educated in secular institutions with minimal exposure to the doctrinal plurality of the classical Islamic sciences and hence prefer clear-cut divisions between right and wrong. Yet ambiguity and contradiction were palpable in Angga's life, since he was homophobic on the one hand, and on the other offered a service centered on penises and men's sexual desires, a business that was quite possibly homoerotic. When I pointed this out, he responded in agitation, "I am a poor person who must do whatever it takes to live in this city! Someone from a developed country could not possibly understand this!" He hastily took leave and stopped corresponding with me for several months, perhaps because he thought I was criticizing him or making an argument about Islamist hypocrisy. I am, however, more interested in what "strange" behaviors like Angga's reveal about the legacies left behind by New Order policies. As a product of a turbulent political context, Angga was shaped by the patterns of religious socialization established by Suharto-era educational reforms as well as by the freedom of individual expression and the freedom of the market in the post-Suharto era. The convergence of these forces in Angga's life produced an unstable religious and secular assemblage that he struggled to hold together.

The seemingly inexplicable is pervasive in Indonesia because of how much the New Order has dominated its political and cultural landscape, which is why scholars and commentators of Indonesia have always stumbled upon incidents, trends, or people that are impossible to account for and cannot be easily categorized (Rutherford 2014; Tagliacozzo 2014).[16] The New Order expertly manipulated paradoxical strategies and simultaneously used techniques of clarity and non-clarity to maintain political order. The government engaged in rigorous classification of legitimate identities and behavior, always requiring, for example, that people have identity cards and permits to prove they were recognized by the authorities. At the same time, authorities often were deliberately vague. To deter crime in the early 1980s, for example, the government shot criminals and left their bodies in the streets, attributing their deaths to "mysterious killers" (Siegel 1998). Such acts of mystery were designed to prevent Indonesians from ever having a clear understanding of the processes that kept them as repressed subjects. In the democratic age, as ordinary citizens sought to uncover the secrets closely guarded by the government, they began to demand widespread transparency and accountability, as the following chapter will show, even in the domain of religion.

3

ACCOUNTING FOR THE SOUL

Pausing in front of a beggar at a train station, Hassan dropped a 1,000 rupiah note (about ten cents) into her outstretched hand. As we walked away, Hassan did what I thought was the most extraordinary thing. He took from his backpack a small notebook to jot down that he had done his charity for the day. The notebook is essentially a rudimentary type of accounting book.[1] On the notebook's cover page, below the blank spaces where he wrote his personal information, is the slogan, "Let's count our deeds before the Day of Judgment arrives."[2] Each page in the notebook consists of accounting tables. The leftmost column lists the acts to be carried out, among which are congregational prayers, reciting and memorizing the Quran, memorizing the sayings of the Prophet Muhammad, nighttime prayers, and fasting on Mondays and Thursdays. In addition to religious rituals, the piety notebook tracks activities not typically defined as religious, like reading and physical exercise. The accounting table also includes small columns where one can write when each act is performed. The quota to be attained is listed at the bottom of the page: to read one section of the Quran per day, to perform nighttime prayers thrice a week, to read books once a week, to exercise once a week, and so on.

When I asked why he recorded the charity transaction, Hassan replied that it was important for there to be "transparency" (*transparansi*) in worship, regardless of whether the acts were big or small. He then narrated a familiar story about President Suharto, the former military general who used tactics of secrecy, corruption, and misinformation to remain in power from 1965 to 1998 (Pemberton 1994). Hassan described Suharto as impious (*tak religius*) for most of his rule—indeed, Suharto was not only nominally Muslim (he preferred Javanese mysticism over orthodox Muslim practices) but also resolutely anti-Islamic (he banned Muslim political parties and routinely imprisoned religious leaders). In 1991, amid rising public discontent against his rule, he suddenly dragged his entire family on a well-publicized pilgrimage to Mecca (*tiba-tiba pergi haji*), transforming himself as he returned home from Suharto to Haji Mohammad Suharto. There was a subsequent Islamic turn in the regime's policies as Suharto appointed Muslim cabinet members and opened Islamic banks (Hefner 2000, 18–19). To court the support of Muslim constituents in shaky political times, Suharto had thus seemingly conjured piety out of thin air. The piety notebook and the *transparansi* it promotes, according to Hassan, were safeguards against such disingenuous religious conduct.

Discourses of transparency have been popularized in political and cultural spheres since Indonesia's transition from authoritarianism to democracy in 1998. An important political development was the establishment in 2002 of the Corruption Eradication Bureau (Komisi Pemberantasan Korupsi), which investigates and prosecutes cases of corruption in government bodies. Widespread calls for truth and authenticity have also been made by ordinary citizens who want the secrets that had been concealed by the Suharto regime to be revealed. Patricia Spyer (2014) observes how such desires have inspired locally made documentaries, like *Mass Grave* (by director Lexy Junior Rambadeta), which examines the exhumation and reburial of victims of the 1965–1966 anticommunist killings orchestrated by Suharto. Yet other films—in particular, according to Mary Steedly (2013b), the horror films that are enjoying a recent revival—speak of the dangers associated with the urge to see and know. Horror films portray the apparition as the sinister other of transparency: ghosts and demons make an appearance in the everyday world because someone is looking for them; but once they are seen, it is too late to escape from them. These recurrent themes in horror films convey to Indonesian audiences that their demands for transparency will inadvertently leave them exposed.

Hassan's piety notebook is rooted in the politics of anticorruption in contemporary Indonesia. He received the notebook as a participant of the conservative Islamist student Campus Proselytization Association, which is affiliated with the Prosperous Justice Party. Influenced by Egypt's Muslim Brotherhood, the Prosperous Justice Party is among the most powerful Islamist political organizations in democratic Indonesia. In 1999, during the first free elections after Suharto's resignation, the party campaigned on distinctive Islamist concerns such as the establishment of an Islamic state and the implementation of sharia law in Indonesia. It won just over 1 percent of total votes. The flop led party leaders to de-emphasize its religiously conservative interests and promote transparency, which they argued was a Muslim virtue. This proved to be a successful electoral strategy: the party obtained between 7 and 8 percent of votes in both the 2004 and 2009 elections, results significant enough for party leaders to be appointed to important ministerial positions. To translate its political ambitions into the level of micropolitics, the party introduced the piety notebook to teach its followers about transparency. Implicit in the Islamist pedagogy, therefore, is the notion that the formation of a democratic social order is deeply intertwined with the formation of the religious self.

The piety notebook is, to invoke the concept developed by Aihwa Ong and Stephen Collier once more, a global assemblage, "the product of multiple determinations that are not reducible to a single logic" (2005, 12). Among such "determinations" are ideas about the accounting of worship in traditional Islamic doctrine. For example, Muslims believe that two angels, Raqib and Atib, sit on each shoulder and record all our thoughts, feelings, and actions. Our good deeds are documented on our right shoulder, the bad ones on the left. The Quran (99, 7–8) states that even the most minuscule of acts—"an atom's weight of good" and "an atom's weight of evil"—will be recorded. On the Day of Judgment, after the entire world is annihilated and all of humanity is resurrected, the angels will present our cumulative deeds to God. This will be the basis of our final reckoning: the righteous will be rewarded with paradise, while the unrighteous will be tortured in hell.

The piety notebook combines the calculative logic internal to Islam with bureaucratic practices of accounting. Accounting has a genealogy to sixteenth-century methods of financial management in Europe. Merchants of the time, generally held in low esteem, adopted statistical innovations like double-entry bookkeeping, which displayed commercial transactions and records of money due and owed, to proclaim mercantile honesty and credibility (Poovey 1998, xvii). By the nineteenth century, statistics were not only valued in business but became increasingly important as a technology of governance in Europe and its colonies as states began to conduct audits and population censuses and compile crime and unemployment rates, under the assumption that such numbers facilitated objective policy decisions (Porter 1995, 35–37). Neoliberal reforms since the 1970s have further intensified reliance on statistics to measure and maximize the quality and value of money by governments, businesses, international governance organizations, and civil society groups. In particular, there has been an "audit explosion" where people check their behavior for themselves so that governments can withdraw from checking behavior and simply check indicators of performance (Strathern 2000). An important theme that emerges from the history of accounting and other statistical measures is the central role they play in cultivating secular liberal values like transparency, objectivity, individual autonomy, and self-help.

Combining disparate regimes of calculation, one rooted in the Islamic tradition and the other in secular liberalism, the piety notebook reveals Islam's ability to absorb forms and practices that are external to it. The piety notebook is simultaneously religious and political, as it imagines that educating young Indonesians to document every single act of piety, even the few cents given to a beggar, is instrumental in leading the nation away from what it was under Suharto. The adaptive capacities embodied by the piety notebook challenge dominant Western assumptions that Islam is antithetical to secular liberalism, which have historically allowed Westerners to justify their rejection of Muslims (Massad 2015). By telling the story of the piety notebook and the conservative Islamists who use it, I hope to show that to be Muslim in the contemporary geopolitical context means having to contend with the hegemony of secular liberalism, even though the adoption of liberal methods does not necessarily transform Muslims into liberal subjects.

Bureaucratic Islamists

I encountered the piety notebook at the Campus Proselytization Association, the most nationally prominent Islamist student organization, which has chapters at major Indonesian universities, including the University of Indonesia, where my research was conducted. I had to overcome several bureaucratic hurdles before gaining access to the organization. I obtained the contact number for a student leader named Rahman, whom I telephoned to seek research permission. He requested a curriculum vitae detailing my biographical information, education, and work experience. The request seemed excessively formal in Indonesia, where I have found it acceptable to make an interview appointment via text message even with prominent politicians. Three weeks after I e-mailed him my curriculum vitae, Rahman asked for additional information, including a description of my research objectives, sample interview questions, and the expected outcomes of the study. It took another two weeks before Rahman allowed my research to proceed. The interaction with Rahman, which made me feel like a job seeker, provided important insight into the uses of bureaucracy by the Islamist movement, of which the piety notebook is just one example.

Typical of a bureaucracy, the Campus Proselytization Association has an office space, a committee of officeholders (the president, vice president, and heads of various departments like research and development, street demonstrations and proselytization strategies, and women's affairs), a logo, and official stationery. Rahman, the public relations head, explained that he was "merely following procedures" (*cuma ikut prosedur*) in his formalistic communication with me, as officeholders have received training on how to communicate as representatives of the organization, including on the proper uses of salutations in a letter and how to sign off. When planning events—which can range from fund-raising to seminars on local and global political issues and campaigns to encourage female undergraduates to put on the head scarf—officeholders consult manuals that have been prepared by alumni participants. These manuals, which are written in Indonesian but peppered with transliteration of business jargon from English, contain instructions such as the following: before each event, officeholders must discuss and decide on the "target object" of the project, the best "product" to be used, the division of labor, the amount of funding, and timeline. In these manuals, a project is often described as "work" that can be best performed when there is "professionalism" and "synergy" between the various departments in the organization.

One of the most important events takes place during the first week of the new academic year, which is when the organization tries to recruit potential members from among the incoming freshmen undergraduates. At this time, the campus would be decorated with banners, posters, and sign-up booths; recruiters from all student organizations prowled the hallways to distribute pamphlets and talk to new students. Since organizations were competing for participants, many recruiters imposed themselves quite aggressively on the freshmen. As we observed recruiters from other organizations pulling reluctant students to the sign-up booths, Rahman informed me, in English this time, that recruiters from the Campus Proselytization Association employed a different "marketing strategy" from the "hard sell" approach of other organizations. "A soft-sell approach is more effective," he said. Rahman explained that the recruiter might break the ice by offering the freshman something to drink, and volunteer to escort the newcomer to the faculty administrative office to complete the freshman registration process. Perhaps the recruiter might also ask if the student wanted to be taken on a campus tour. Only when rapport is established between the recruiter and the freshman would information about the organization be given. The success of this strategy, according to Rahman, accounts for why the Campus Proselytization Association is the largest student organization at the university.[3]

When an event has concluded, officeholders must prepare a report describing the event, how the officers prepared for it, the number of committee members present at meetings, and an evaluation of staff performance. The report Rahman wrote for the student recruitment event also included an analysis of "SWOT" factors, or Strengths, Weaknesses, Opportunities, and Threats, derived from a strategic planning method created by the management consultant Albert Humphrey to identify the objectives of a project and the factors that are favorable or unfavorable to the accomplishment of those aims. Once completed, a report must be archived along with supplementary materials like photographs. All expenditure must be substantiated with receipts submitted to the organization's treasurer, so as to ensure, as Rahman joked, "that no one stole any money."

The adoption of bureaucracy and other corporate practices by the organization should be seen in relation to the evolving role of bureaucracy in Indonesia. According to Karen Strassler (2010), bureaucracy was central to the surveillance apparatus of the New Order. During its rule, citizens had to carry at all times official forms of identification, the most important of which were identity cards. The identity card contained a photograph of its holder, which "became an idiomatic shorthand for the state's assertion of its own power to authenticate who was a citizen and who fell outside the fold of state recognition and protection" (138). While the identity photograph seemed to impose a secular national identity, the state also enforced religiosity by requiring an inclusion of religious affiliation from the five officially recognized religions: Islam, Protestant Christianity, Catholicism, Hinduism, and Buddhism. Strassler notes that the Chinese minority were subjected to additional bureaucratic scrutiny, as they had to carry not only their identity cards but also a proof-of-citizenship letter to ensure they were not foreigners. As this letter could be requested at any moment, Chinese Indonesians were often vulnerable to bribe solicitation by bureaucrats.

Though associated with the panoptic vision and corruption of the Suharto regime, bureaucracy acquired new uses and meanings following the regime's ouster. The beginning of the end for Suharto could be traced to the events of 1997, when Indonesia was plunged into an economic crisis that caused massive unemployment and bankruptcy. Although the causes of the collapse are complex, a consensus reached by economists is that Indonesia had borrowed at unsustainable rates in the pre-crisis period. Citizens across Indonesia, led by students and the civil society, mobilized in fervent protests against *korupsi, kolusi, nepotisme* (corruption, collusion, nepotism), or how the system of patronage created many competing interests that prevented the regime from acting decisively in a crisis. Anger toward the government was also directed at the ethnic Chinese, who were seen as Suharto's cronies, resulting in the looting of Chinese-owned stores and the rapes of Chinese women. Suharto stepped down in May 1998, after the prolonged demonstrations and rioting by dissatisfied citizens made it evident that the regime could no longer restore political stability.

With Suharto's resignation, Indonesia entered into a period of wide-ranging social, political, and economic reforms that Indonesians call

Reformasi. Economically, the International Monetary Fund bailed out the Indonesian economy, which resulted in the privatization of state-owned enterprises and growth in foreign investment and the manufacturing sector (Rudnyckyj 2010, 69). Such interventions by international governance organizations have historically been crucial in bringing neoliberalism to the global South (Goldman 2007).[4] It is well known by now that neoliberalism is a technique of governing in which people are expected to be free and self-managing in their lives, including but not limited to education, work, and health care, as a response to the freeing of global markets from governmental intervention (Harvey 2005). Importantly, neoliberal reforms in Indonesia occurred alongside the democratization of the polity. Transparency and anticorruption became central governmental concerns, and a renewed emphasis was placed on audits—for example, the State Audit Law passed in 2004 provides the State Audit Agency (Badan Pemeriksa Keuangan) with a mandate to audit all public institutions. These attempts to check and curb governmental power in the realm of economics and politics suggest that there has been a spread of the neoliberal discourse of "responsibilization," or the notion that individuals are responsible for their own care and advancement (Rose 1999).

In this context, bureaucracy began to be utilized in neoliberal and democratic ways by Indonesians, suggesting that it has moved beyond the singular frame of governmental surveillance. Karen Strassler observes a new political consciousness—the emergence of a "culture of documentation," as seen in the rise of photography exhibitions chronicling Suharto's overthrow, as well as debates on the importance of producing alternative documents to correct the state's version of history (2010, 16). Daromir Rudnyckyj (2004), on the other hand, analyzes how private companies rely on bureaucracy to inculcate the work ethic. He discusses how human resources companies use score sheets (measuring qualities like concentration, work motivation, and self-confidence) and regimented daily schedules as "technologies of servitude" aimed to endow women with skills to work as maids outside Indonesia. Databases were also used by these companies to keep track of domestic workers as they venture abroad for work. These surveillance systems, aimed at preventing the abuse of maids by their employers, are an implicit criticism of the Indonesian government's failure to offer adequate protection to these workers.

Indonesia's political and economic reforms took place alongside an Islamic religious revitalization, where there has been an unprecedented engagement with religious texts by Muslims who were not necessarily educated at Islamic religious institutions (Hefner and Horvatich 1997). Religious practices in this context became influenced by the repurposing of bureaucracy as well as the uptake of other corporate technologies in projects of responsibilization. Like the piety notebook, many of these religious innovations are global assemblages in their own right. Studying a steel factory that recently underwent privatization, Daromir Rudnyckyj (2010) observes the participation of its workers in the Emotional and Spiritual Quotient (ESQ) program. Conducted by spiritual trainers, ESQ teaches a form of Islam that is conducive to both personal growth and business success in order to create individual workers who are simultaneously pious and productive. Similarly, James Hoesterey (2016) examines the rise of new Muslim preachers who combine religious teachings with messages about popular psychology and self-help and who have become popular among middle-class Indonesians.

The piety notebook and other bureaucratic practices in the Campus Proselytization Association appeared during the intense social, political, and economic reforms in post-Suharto Indonesia, and were thus influenced by the dominant discourses of the day. As previously mentioned, the Campus Proselytization Association is the student affiliate of the Prosperous Justice Party. Formed after Suharto's ouster, the Prosperous Justice Party competed in the 1999 elections, proposing to establish an Islamic state in Indonesia. After the party managed to attract just over 1 percent of total votes, party leaders moderated their stance regarding the implementation of the sharia, arguing that the sharia should not be applied at the symbolic level, but at the practical level through the enforcement of good governance. With the slogan "clean, caring, and professional" (*bersih, peduli, profesional*), the party turned its focus to issues of the feeble economy and rampant corruption (Hasan 2009). The party has the greatest support among young, educated, and urban voters, in part because of its efforts to reach out to university students via the Campus Proselytization Association. It is through the student organization, where the piety notebook and other bureaucratic practices are introduced, that the party seeks to groom subjects suited for Indonesia's new democratic and neoliberal era—individuals who are pious, responsibilized, and auditable.

The Study Circle

Much of my fieldwork was spent in study circles (*liqo*), where I observed the use of the piety notebook. While the Campus Proselytization Association organizes many activities—including lectures, camps, and excursions—the study circle is the most intensive pedagogical site. Each study circle consists of between five and twelve participants. Discussions are led by a mentor (the English term is used interchangeably with its Arabic translation *murobi*), typically a more advanced undergraduate. Participants and their mentor are of the same gender. Study circles meet weekly for one and a half to two hours, typically at the University of Indonesia's campus mosque. Located beside a lake at the center of the campus, the mosque is an important social space for Muslim undergraduates who come not only to pray, but also to meet friends, borrow books at the Islamic library, or take naps. Islamist students, however, stake a special claim over the mosque, as the Campus Proselytization Association is the only student organization with an office at the mosque. Male study circles meet at the first floor near the male prayer hall, while female groups meet near the female prayer hall at the mezzanine.

I participated in an all-male study circle consisting of eight freshmen and their mentor, Jamal, a senior undergraduate. The members of the study circle joined the organization for a variety of reasons. One wished to depart from a teenage life of fun and impiety—he used to "go to the clubs too often" (*sering dugem*)—and sought to deepen his understanding of Islam. Some students, including Jamal, recognized that the organization is a good place to make friends, especially if, like Jamal, they are not from Jakarta and do not have a readily accessible social network, while others are inspired by the long history of student activism in Indonesia and want to contribute to social and political causes (see also Lee 2016). Similarly, in her study of the recent proliferation of Islamic dress in Indonesia, Carla Jones (2007) argues that Muslim women embrace modesty fashion for multiple reasons, including wanting to be more accountable to God, to become a modern and stylish individual, and to enhance personal security in morally fraught, male-dominated workplaces. Religious motivations are indeed complex, as Saba Mahmood notes when she takes Pierre Bourdieu to task for treating bodily practices, including religious practices, as simply an index of class habitus (Mahmood 2005, 26).

From the beginning of my study, I was struck by Jamal's effort to maintain an atmosphere of seriousness. There was a student who fancied himself a jester and often told silly jokes. While other participants and I could hardly contain our laughter, Jamal constantly kept a grave face and reminded everyone that humor had no place in the group. When I asked Jamal privately how he managed to remain so stoic in the face of laughter, he said that he had undergone mentor training (conducted by party cadres) where he was taught to anticipate such behavior. He showed me an instructional guide that had been distributed to all mentors. "If your student makes a joke and you cannot contain yourself, suppress your laughter and instead give a voiceless smile," the guidebook says. "After all, Prophet Muhammad dislikes exaggerated and over-the-top humor." The guidebook is not concerned with humor per se but with disruptive behavior more generally. Mentors are tasked not only to eliminate jokes, but also to quickly resolve conflicts that may arise between participants or between a participant and the mentor. Troublemakers were to be reported to the leaders of the Campus Proselytization Association and transferred to another study circle. Such practices thus allow for the containment of potentially disruptive situations so that the study circle can accomplish its main objective: to inculcate discipline.

To form disciplined subjects, the study circle follows a curriculum designed by the Prosperous Justice Party. Broadly speaking, the readings in the curriculum fall into two subject matters:

1. Islamic theology. Topics include the characteristics of Allah, the characteristics of the Prophet Muhammad, the foundations of Islamic teachings, the Islamic concept of monotheism, and features of the afterlife. Participants read works by authoritative classical scholars including *The Revival of the Religious Sciences* by Imam al-Ghazali (d. 1111) and *The Gardens of the Righteous* by Imam Nawawi (d. 1277), as well as various works by Muslim Brotherhood theologians like Said Hawwa and Muhammad Qutb, and other prominent Islamists such as Abul A'la Maududi.
2. Political mobilization. Themes include the characteristics and strategies of Islamic proselytization (*da'wa*), ideological battles in Islam (*ghazw al-fikri*), Islam's enemies (Zionists have been identified as a primary enemy), and youth contributions to Islamic proselytization.

While many readings classified under Islamic theology are conventional from the perspective of traditional seminary education, the readings for political mobilization are unique to Islamists. In addition to studying the political writings of Muslim Brotherhood thinkers like Hasan al-Banna, the students also read the works of local Islamist authors, as well as publications by the World Assembly of Muslim Youth (an international youth organization that has come under scrutiny for its links to the bin Laden family). All readings are read in the Indonesian translations, as most participants do not have Arabic proficiency. While the writings of Islamist authors were banned during the Suharto regime, today they can be obtained easily in the numerous independent bookstores located around campus.

Each meeting begins with a group recitation of Quranic verses for about fifteen minutes, followed by an hour-long discussion of the assigned text. Jamal frames the discussion by first lecturing on the text, usually for twenty minutes or so. Like most participants, I take copious notes during lectures. The summary of the notes I took during a lecture on classical scholar al-Ghazali's most famous work, *Ihya Ulum ad-Din* (Revival of the religious sciences), is as follows: "Al-Ghazali's theory of knowledge is that all knowledge is revealed by God to humans via prophets. Revealed knowledge will enable humans to take in God's divine essence and fulfill their potential. Since prophets are transmitters of revealed knowledge, we should imitate their behaviors in order for us to purify our hearts, eliminate our negative qualities, and take in the revealed knowledge. Muslims must emulate Muhammad in particular, since he is not only our prophet but also God's last messenger to humankind. Those who refuse must surely be under the influence of Satan."

Following each lecture, Jamal would open the floor for discussion for about thirty minutes. Unlike in academic settings, the participants were not especially concerned with dissecting texts with scholarly or theoretical interest. Texts were regarded as normative, since they were written by those considered religious authorities. As such, discussions were usually centered on how the arguments of the texts could be implemented in the participants' lives. After the lecture on al-Ghazali that I summarized earlier, the group launched into a conversation on how to emulate the Prophet

Muhammad. The participants tossed up some ideas: people should follow how he worshipped, or how he interacted with people, or even his personal grooming habits. Saba Mahmood (2009) theorizes such behavior among Muslims using the Aristotelian concept of *schesis*: that Muslims demonstrate their love and devotion to their Prophet by inhabiting his persona. This is why Muslims reacted so angrily toward satirical cartoons of the Prophet published in the Danish newspaper *Jyllands-Posten* in 2006 or the French magazine *Charlie Hebdo* in 2015. While not breaking any laws, the cartoons transgressed the habitus of Muslims and were taken as personal insults.

The participants in the study circle quickly discovered, however, that it is difficult to imitate the Prophet. Specifically, they found trouble with two embodied practices. First, the participants were encouraged to fold the hem of their trousers so as to reveal their ankles, given that a hadith says, "As narrated by 'Abdullah bin 'Umar, Allah's Apostle said: 'Allah will not look at the person who drags his garment [behind him] out of conceit.' "[5] There are unending disagreements among Muslims whether the hadith is a criticism of long garments per se or whether it is actually about arrogance and opulent behavior, but Islamists take the literal interpretation. A few participants who began to raise the hemline of their trousers sheepishly reported that they were subjected to teasing or sarcastic remarks from their family and friends. "Why are your pants so short? Must be flooding in Jakarta right now!" reported a student on the remark that he heard most frequently (which is a reference to the seasonal floods that affect the city annually).

Second, the participants were encouraged to grow a beard, given that a hadith says, "As narrated by Ibn 'Umar, Allah's Apostle said, 'Cut the moustaches short and leave the beard [as it is].' "[6] However, most of these eighteen- and nineteen-year-olds were simply unable to grow facial hair. "It would take me weeks before I see a stubble on my chin," one of them lamented. "I don't even own a shaver," another smooth-faced student confessed. Whenever the students brought up the difficulties they encountered in inhabiting the Prophet's persona, Jamal would tell them, "Don't be discouraged, and keep on trying!" He reminded them of how the pagans of Mecca taunted, criticized, and eventually waged battles against the Prophet when he preached the message of monotheism. Just as the

Prophet persisted in the face of adversity, they too should do the same and continue to wear pants with hemlines shortened and attempt to grow a beard regardless of the challenges they faced.

"You will be rewarded for following in the footsteps of the Prophet" (Mengikuti sunnah nabi akan mendapatkan pahala), Jamal often said, adding that there is even a hadith pronouncing that those who stead-fastly emulate the Prophet in times of difficulty will earn fifty times more merit. Jamal's message reflects ideas about calculation that are present in Islamic religious practices. There are authoritative doctrines proposing that merit can be added, subtracted (when counterbalanced by sin), and even multiplied (as some acts are worth more than others—for example, prayers performed during Lailatul Qadar, the Night of Power occurring the last ten days of Ramadan when the Prophet ascended to heaven, are said to be the equivalent of worship in one thousand months). While the accrual of merit is an incentive, Jamal discouraged the students from being instrumentalist. "We should not discriminate between good acts" (Kita tidak harus membeda-bedakan amal), he said to deter them from per-forming acts that are weightier in merit at the expense of quotidian ones. He added, "People who do that don't have pure intentions in worship" (Orang yang seperti itu niatnya tidak tulus), to underscore that sincerity depends on a holistic submission to religion.

The pedagogy in the study circle bears some resemblance to the self-cultivation model proposed by Talal Asad (1986), Charles Hirsch-kind (2006), and Saba Mahmood (2005). To recap, the self-cultivation model argues that discipline works differently in Islam compared to how it works in the secular liberal West. On the one hand, Islamists do use technologies of the self that "permit individuals to effect by their own means or with the help of others a certain number of operations on their own bodies and souls, thoughts, conduct, and a way of being, so as to transform themselves in order to attain a certain state of happiness, purity, wisdom, perfection, or immortality" (Foucault 1988, 18). On the other hand, these technologies of the self do not help them become self-owning liberal subjects but instead mold them into religious subjects defined in re-lation to the Quran and the Prophet. Thus, the study circle is not similar to the Western reading public described by Jürgen Habermas (1962), where rational individuals engage one another in reasoned debate. Instead, the study circle resembles what Hirschkind calls the "Islamic counter-public" where persuasion occurs not through rational deliberation but by the disciplined cultivation of certain habits of the heart and the body.

Progression

"Everyone, please take out your notebooks," Jamal would announce toward the conclusion of each study circle meeting. He would then check whether the participants had managed to attain the quota of piety acts expected of them (to read one section of the Quran per day, to perform nighttime prayers thrice a week, and so on). If a participant missed the quota once, Jamal would simply remind him not to be so lax. If a participant missed the quota on a regular basis, Jamal might ask the young man's friends to send him daily piety reminders through text messaging or invite him to perform the rituals together. If peer pressure failed, the offender would be brought before more senior figures in the Islamist movement (usually a middle-aged religious teacher) to be chastised. The use of accounting and auditing to groom self-governing believers suggests that while there are distinctively Muslim modalities of discipline at work, Islamist pedagogy is also moored to the ideals of Western democracy. The hybrid character of Islamist socialization reflects how secular liberalism has become hegemonic in the modern world to the extent that even these conservative Muslims cannot avoid it altogether.

The piety notebook mainly serves as a metric for determining whether students can progress to more advanced study circles, where they will be exposed to more sophisticated pedagogical literature. Decisions on advancement are made at the end of the academic year, where the numbers in the piety notebook are examined alongside other indicators, including the scores for the quizzes that students take on the reading materials, the number of Quranic verses memorized, and the grade-point average for their coursework. Yet how exactly these numbers are compiled to determine a satisfactory grade for promotion is unclear to me and the participants, or even to the mentor himself. Procedurally, Jamal reports these various indicators to the leaders of the Campus Proselytization Association, who after some time will convey their findings to the participants. This is typical of accounting regimes where transparency is expected of the audited subjects but not the assessors. The decision of the leaders is largely predictable: everyone passes and can be promoted to a higher-level study circle. It is not in the interest of the organization to fail anyone and risk losing participants (as it is, it is common for students to quit once they lose interest). Rather, there is greater incentive for the organization to retain participants and continuously groom them into Islamist subjects.

If indicators are utilized perfunctorily in the promotion of the participants, they play a more significant role in the selection of officeholders. To understand this process, we must first understand that the Campus Proselytization Association has what its leaders call "a methodical socialization system" (*system kaderisasi yang metodik*) that consists of two parallel hierarchies. The first, the piety hierarchy, consists of different levels of study circles in which one consumes more advanced pedagogical materials the higher one travels up the structure (*usroh yang bertahap*). Alongside the piety hierarchy is the administrative hierarchy, or the ordering of political rank in the organization in which ordinary members (or participants without administrative responsibilities) are at the very bottom (*pengkaderan kepemimpinan yang bertahap*). As participants move up the piety hierarchy, they can also theoretically move up the administrative hierarchy. For example, as freshmen participants progress continuously to higher study circles, they can be promoted from an ordinary member of the organization to membership on subcommittees and main committees. Once Jamal advanced to a higher-level study circle, he was selected to join the teaching and pedagogy committee, which was how he became the mentor of a study circle.

The piety hierarchy has primacy over its administrative counterpart, as it is the piety rank that determines administrative rank and not vice versa. One cannot assume a more important bureaucratic position without first becoming more pious in the Islamist rubric. Additionally, the more important the bureaucratic position a participant occupies, the better that person's piety indicators are expected to be. A piety indicator used to determine preparedness for leadership roles relates to the Quran. The Quran is divided into thirty parts of equal length that are called *juz*. Quranic recitation is often structured around the *juz*: during Ramadan, for example, many ordinary Muslims recite one *juz* per night so as to complete the entire Quran by the end of the fasting month. Conservative Islamists are, however, expected to go beyond recitation and know the Quran by heart. Regular boot camps are organized by the Campus Proselytization

Association to help its participants memorize verses by the *juz*. People inform me that the key officeholders of the organization are expected to memorize one *juz*, while the chairperson has to memorize more, some say five *juz*.

The Campus Proselytization Association is connected to the Prosperous Justice Party through the piety and administrative hierarchies. Following their graduation from university, many members of the student organization will continue to participate in the Islamist study circles and hence maintain their progress up the piety ladder. This is because they remain in the Islamist orbit after leaving university, finding employment in the social services organizations that have been established by the Prosperous Justice Party. Examples include philanthropic associations that oversee the collection and disbursement of the tithe (*zakat*), cooperatives that give out interest-free loans for small businesses, and schools (from kindergarten to high schools) with a hybrid Islamic-secular curriculum. Regarded by the Prosperous Justice Party as supplementary venues for exerting its political influence, these social services organizations also represent the neoliberal trend where the responsibility for providing essential goods and services is increasingly shouldered by the civil society (Ferguson and Gupta 2002). Employees in these organizations form study circles that meet in an office premises, a mosque, a participant's home, or even at cafés and bistros in downtown Jakarta.

A young politician who was a former student activist in the Campus Proselytization Association described the Prosperous Justice Party as "a party of ideas, not personality."[7] In our interview, the politician demonstrated fluency in English as well as, to my astonishment, familiarity with Max Weber's theories (cf. Gerth and Mills 1946). He explained that the party nurtures "bureaucratic authority" over "charismatic authority," rationalizing that whereas the former creates efficiency, a party that relies on the charisma of its leader cannot survive the downfall of the leader. The politician's trust in bureaucracy is similarly embodied by the Campus Proselytization Association's promotional system, where continuous participation in study circles following graduation allows young Islamists to ascend the party's administrative hierarchy. Specifically, they can become an officeholder in the party, first at the subdistrict level, and if the upward movement proceeds unabated, subsequently at the district level, the province level, and finally the headquarters. This bureaucratic design encapsulates the Islamist vision on how to transform post-Suharto Indonesia: Piety, which will be cultivated through accounting and numerically quantified, should be rewarded with political positions. In turn, these pious political leaders will theoretically weed out the corruption endemic to the nation and spearhead Indonesia's spiritual regeneration.

"Democracy is the best system for Indonesia right now, but it doesn't always fulfill its promises," said the politician as he bemoaned the failure of the country's nascent democracy to address rampant corruption, widespread poverty, and low educational standards. As an Islamist politician, he aimed to "make democracy better" by supplementing it with Islam so that politicians are held accountable to God. In wanting to blend Islam and secular liberalism, the politician shows that Islamist beliefs are hardly rigid but are in fact contingent on the ever-shifting contexts in which Islamists live. In her study of a cancer ward in Botswana, Julie Livingston (2012) discusses medical care that is contingent upon whether vital machines are working properly, whether bed space is available, whether drugs are in or out of stock—consequently, medicine is "improvised" because doctors constantly have to ad lib and resort to ad hoc measures. Similarly, I describe the religious behavior that I study as improvisational, to draw attention to the element of unpredictability at work. In other words, Islamists have embraced bureaucracy to promote piety and transparency in post-Suharto Indonesia—but does their improvisational project achieve its intended outcomes?

Unstable Assemblages

Clear-cut plans do not necessarily produce clear-cut results, particularly if the plans rely on the foreseeable workings of a global assemblage. I have made the case that the piety notebook is a global assemblage formed at the nexus of multiple factors. The first, accounting and auditing, have become widespread in neoliberal governmental policy making, as they allow ordinary people to check their behavior for themselves so that governments can withdraw from checking behavior and simply check indicators of performance (Merry 2016). Despite the recent popularity of accounting and auditing, Western governments have used statistical information (like the census) to make policy decisions since the eighteenth century. In her analysis of nineteenth-century British governmental documents, Mary Poovey (1998) observes that the texts tended to combine numerical tables on urban squalor with a narrative commentary of those neighborhoods. Poovey argues that the separation of one mode of representation—the numbers—from another—the narrative commentary—reflects the epistemological belief that numbers stood apart from interpretation or subjective remarks. It is this presumption that numbers were neutral and immune to biases that made them so foundational to liberal democracies.

The piety notebook also draws on Muslim beliefs about the accounting of worship—for example, that all human merits and sins are recorded by angels and presented to God on the Day of Judgment. When I posed a question about how these angels worked, Jamal replied, "A hadith states that the angels delay the recording of a bad deed for six hours. If we regret a bad deed and repent within the six-hour window, then it will not be recorded. If we regret a bad deed after it has been recorded but repent before our death, then the bad deed could be erased. Even if we did not repent, God may still grant us mercy because he is all-forgiving." Jamal's account reflects a traditional view within Islam where deeds are not necessarily fixed, unchangeable, or commensurable units. Muslim tabulation of deeds is different from the secular liberal regime of calculation informing the actions of, say, French state engineers in the 1830s, to cite an example discussed by Sally Merry (2011, S85). These engineers began planning for transportation infrastructure by first measuring public utility, an indicator of the benefits of public goods balanced against their monetary cost. Making decisions on the basis of calculation enabled the engineers to avoid problems of corruption and prejudice that might otherwise influence the locations of the roads and railways they were building. In contrast to the Muslims, therefore, the engineers regarded numbers as objective entities.

Traditional Muslim doctrine also posits that piety will not necessarily be rewarded with material gains in the secular world. During a meeting discussing "the fundamentals of Islamic teachings" (*pokok-pokok ajaran Islam*), Jamal stated that the remuneration for worship will come only in the afterlife. This implies that the material wealth one accumulates in this world does not necessarily indicate the attainment of God's favor. In fact, Jamal added, the Quran states that wealth is actually a test for human beings: "Verily! We have made that which is on earth an adornment for it, in order that We may test them [mankind] as to which of them are best in deeds" (Q 18, 7). Material accumulation is considered to be so dangerous that God exhorts Muslims to give away what they have through charity. Jamal cited another verse to emphasize the point: "They ask you (O Muhammad) what they should spend. Say: Whatever you spend of good must be for parents and kindred and orphans and the poor and the wayfarer; and whatever you do of good deeds, truly, Allah knows it well" (Q 2, 215).

In contrast, the piety notebook establishes a correlation between piety and secular rewards. Material incentives for the attainment of positive piety indicators come in the form of administrative positions in the organization, which often translate into future internships and jobs in the Prosperous Justice Party and affiliated institutions. The promise of job security is not a trivial one for Indonesian students, who like other youths must grapple with the contemporary global economy and constantly worry about postgraduation job prospects. Furthermore, participants in the Campus Proselytization Association were regularly told that secular accomplishments were no less important than piety. Participants were expected to maintain a minimum GPA of 3.0 for their coursework and would be offered tutoring should their grades slip. Mock job interviews would be organized for graduating seniors, who were also encouraged to read popular management books like *The Leader in You*, and *How to Win Friends and Influence People*, both written by the American self-help guru Dale Carnegie. Periodically, announcements would be circulated on current and former students who managed to get on the dean's list, win prestigious scholarships and national competitions, get good jobs, and enter graduate schools.

Jamal worried that the piety notebook creates the possibility for chicanery.[8] He discovered that the students go to great lengths to create justifiable methods to make up for pious acts they missed. For example, if a student failed to recite one section of the Quran on a particular day, he may read extra sections the next day. Alternatively, he may perform charitable acts (for example, by giving money to a beggar) and regard it as sufficient atonement for the missed recitation. The students did not consider these compensatory measures cheating, citing a jurisprudential concept called *qada. Qada* outlines how one can make up for the pious acts that one has missed because of situations of duress, such as illness or travel. Reasoning that their packed schedules should be regarded as duress, the students argued that *qada* is a legitimate recourse for them. Despite Jamal's concerns about the students' sincerity in worship, sincerity is not necessarily inimical to instrumentalist acts. In her study of the Suharto regime's efforts to promote Quranic learning and recitation, Anna Gade (2004) describes the emotional transformation of individuals who spend long hours reciting and memorizing the Quran, suggesting that socially constructed emotions played an equal role to the state's strategy in shaping these Muslims. In contrast, Jamal was suspicious of strategy and warned the students that while they might be able deceive him by fudging their numbers, they would not be able to hoodwink God.

Another concern that I often heard from the students is that measuring piety with simplified numbers and rewarding it with promotion might not result in the most desirable outcomes. Ahmad, the chairperson of the Campus Proselytization Association, was a popular topic of these grumblings. To become chairperson, he had to distinguish himself by attaining the highest piety ratings, including memorizing the most number of Quranic *juz*. By and large, I perceived him to be a capable leader: in our interviews, he demonstrated good knowledge of the history of the organization and the sociology of its participants, and a clearly articulated vision of the organization's future direction. However, he could never answer my inquires about female participants and typically directed me to Amina, the head of women's affairs. His uncertainty about the organization's women would always exasperate Amina, who had made it a point to update him regularly about women's activities. She felt that a good leader should be concerned about women, a criteria she felt Ahmad did not fulfill. Amina's criticisms of Ahmad could be read as an indictment of how the organization's technical method of selecting leaders sacrifices nuance and depth.

Instead of transparency, therefore, the piety notebook resulted in widespread attempts by the students to game the quota as well as losses in subtlety when choosing leaders. Scholars have argued that quantification practices often fail to produce the anticipated outcomes because they promote awareness of the rules of calculation and how to attain the expected standards. This is why, for instance, there are numerous scandals involving universities that manipulate indicators to improve their rankings (Tuchman 2009). Another reason is that numbers are not neutral and carry certain assumptions, which render certain things visible and others invisible. In her study of British attempts to quantify and enhance productivity among professors, Marilyn Strathern (2000) discovers that because only certain things count as productivity, a result is fatigue and mistrust among the faculty rather than improved performance. These slippages involving the piety notebook and other projects of quantification call into question popular assumptions regarding neoliberal inevitability, or how easily people are transformed into autonomous subjects by neoliberal programs. As Marina Welker (2014) argues, neoliberal projects are often unpredictable. She describes how mining giant Newmont conducts training for Indonesian farmers to encourage them to work harder on their lands (rather than protesting the company's activities), but instead leads to the farmers seeing themselves as entitled to increased support from the company.

My ethnographic observations offer insight into the reversal of fortunes that have befallen the Islamist movement in Indonesia. The movement embraced bureaucratic and neoliberal technologies to create responsibilized subjects and eradicate corruption in Indonesian political culture. It is the movement's framing of transparency as Muslim virtue that contributed to its spectacular rise in the early post-authoritarian years. In the 2014 elections, however, the Prosperous Justice Party stumbled. It won less than 7 percent of votes and ended up in seventh position of twelve competing parties. Consequently, the party suffered a decline in the number of legislators in the House of Representatives and was excluded from the ruling coalition. Observers have attributed the party's poor electoral performance in 2014 to the fact that several of its political leaders were involved in high-profile corruption scandals, the most prominent of which was a case involving the agricultural minister accepting bribes from a company in exchange for a higher beef import quota. While corruption has complex explanations, one plausible cause could be the failures resulting from an organizational culture that links piety and power through quantification. This could be why there are now fierce internal debates about whether to decouple the cultivation of piety from the attainment of political power—and whether the Islamist movement should focus on Indonesia's spiritual reform instead of seizing the state (Muhtadi 2012).

Critics of the Islamist movement have used its recent misfortunes to make an argument about the untrustworthiness of Islamists. They portray the Islamist enterprise as essentially a sham, as not really committed to the nascent Indonesian democracy. Underpinning these criticisms are the assumptions that have become so powerful today: that conservative

Islamists are rigid and inflexible and cannot possibly be compatible with the ideals of secular liberalism. There is some basis for such concerns. Suharto's ouster enabled a plethora of Islamist groups to emerge on the scene, among whom were radical vigilantes who sought to implement sharia law through the use of violence and coercion (Bruinessen 2013). Scholars have shown that these radicals were cultivated by the military and other political factions associated with the Suharto regime that were attempting to regain the power and influence they had lost (Jahroni 2004). In this regard, the religious and political vision of the vigilantes is contingent upon the authoritarian behavior of secular forces who wish to shape Indonesian democracy. These radicals show that Indonesian democracy, just like democracy in the West, is fragile and vulnerable to capture by illiberal actors.

It is important, however, that we not paint all Islamists with a broad brush and assume that they are all antidemocratic. The radicals have objectives and methods that are different from those of the Islamists of my study, who find themselves having to reconcile their desires for piety with popular discourses on transparency. While Robert Hefner (2000) has importantly examined how Muslim progressives reconcile Islam and democracy, producing what he terms "civil Islam," my study suggests that Muslim conservatives are also grappling with the diffusion of democratic ideals. Religion is subsequently improvised as the Islamists embrace bureaucratic and neoliberal technologies to invent hybrid religious forms like the piety notebook. The Indonesian Islamists represent a rising global trend among Muslim conservatives who are utilizing accounting and auditing in their religious projects (Mittermaier 2013). The trust they place in such methods is especially striking to me as I write this book in the United States following the installation of the Trump administration. The administration appears to disavow bureaucratic rationality, for example, when it expresses suspicions over the "true" political leanings of federal employees, places government agencies in the hands of the very people who have vowed to close those agencies, and brandishes proposals to "deconstruct the administrative state."

Despite the enthusiastic turn to accounting and auditing, the Islamists do not necessarily achieve the transparency they desired or become a "facsimile of a Western original" (Hefner 2000, 13). These slippages teach us that encounters between religion and other domains may not produce a perfect portmanteau outcome but instead create emergent and unintended consequences. I have focused on the instabilities that come about from the use of the piety notebook, a global assemblage containing "inherent tensions: global implies broadly encompassing, seamless, and mobile; assemblage implies heterogeneous, contingent, unstable, partial, and situated" (Ong and Collier 2005, 12). Furthermore, as scholars of quantification and other projects of responsibilization have argued, the neoliberal programs that the piety notebook hopes to emulate are rife with tensions and contradictions and often fail. Given such critiques, we could perhaps read the rise and fall of the Islamists in Indonesia's democratic era not as a story of the liberal antipathy of the Islamists, but perhaps as a story of the faith that Islamists place in liberal methods that ultimately forsake them.

4

PLAYING WITH SCRIPTURES

A small two-story house not far from the State Islamic University serves as the headquarters for students who meet regularly to discuss religion and politics. The young men and women in the collective, whose name is Formaci, form autodidactic study circles that consist at times of as few as five people to at other times as many as thirty or more. All the participants have extensive experience in the study of Islam, having enrolled in madrasas since an early age and majoring in subjects like Islamic philosophy, Islamic law, and Islamic theological sciences at the university. They have competence in authoritative religious scriptures and therefore do not include them in their reading list. Instead, they primarily study texts written by the great thinkers from the West, from ancient scholars like Plato and Aristotle to more modern ones like Locke, Hegel, Marx, and Derrida. Their reading habits allow them to formulate an interpretation of Islamic scriptures that upholds democracy, civil liberties, human rights, and gender equality as core values in the religion. They call themselves liberal Muslims, a label that is meant to reflect their progressive politics as well as their efforts to find commensurability between Islam and secular liberalism.

Instead of occupying the solemn learning environment often associated with libraries, madrasas, or university lecture halls, the group conducts its highly intellectual activities in what could be described as a rowdy fraternity house. The eight male participants who live on the second floor not only pay the rent but also set the tone for the entire house. Their lack of interest in housekeeping, for example, is palpable in the downstairs living room where the study circles meet—there are cigarette butts everywhere, as though the floor also serves as an ashtray. Study circles are often interspersed with impromptu card games, jokes, poetry contests, confessions about romantic happiness and sorrows, and the strumming of guitars and the singing of songs. Such activities, which can start in the day and extend till late nights, annoy the neighbors and often deter female participation in the group. Social conventions frown upon young women who keep company with raucous young men, even more so if the men are seemingly prone to antireligious behavior. Once, after a study circle had concluded, I asked Rizal to translate an Arabic word that had entered the discussion. "Arabic is such a rubbish language [*bahasa sampah*]," he replied dismissively and in contradistinction to the reverent Muslim attitude toward the language of the Quran and the Prophet Muhammad. "Poor Muslims are stuck with it."

The activities and behavior of Formaci's participants defy popular narratives about Islam and its scriptures. Discourses about "Islamic terrorism" that have become powerful since 9/11 locate the roots of violence in Islamic scriptures and assume that the Quran compels Muslims to be guided by such scriptures—that the text is agentive, while the reader is passive. In contrast, as Talal Asad has observed, there is an assumption that Christians and Jews are free to interpret the Bible as they please, which means that the reader is conceptualized as actively constructing the meaning of texts in relation to social contexts while the texts themselves are passive. Such double standards should not exist. Asad points out that in Islam, as in other religions, "the way people engage in such complex and multifaceted texts, translating their sense and relevance, is a complicated business involving disciplines and traditions of reading, personal habit, and temperament, as well as the perceived demands of particular social situations" (2003, 10–11). Indeed, all texts exist in complex interpretive relationships with historically situated audiences, as Laura Bohannan (1966) has shown in her classic essay *Shakespeare in the Bush*. Attempting to tell the story of Hamlet to the Tiv of Western Africa, Bohannan struggles to explain European concepts of the supernatural, kinship, and justice to the Tiv, who, guided by their own cultural frameworks, emerge with a different understanding of the Shakespearean play. In a delightful reversal of roles, the Tiv even suggested that Bohannan misunderstood Hamlet's story and advise her to consult her own elders at home.

There are multiple historical factors permitting Formaci's participants to read scripture through the lens of Western humanities and social sciences and arrive at a liberal interpretation. On the one hand, the enterprise undertaken by the liberal Muslims in Formaci is not exactly new. Scholars have long described Indonesia as a deeply plural society with multiple modes of religious governance and political organization that have led to alternative ideas on how to be Muslim. Dealing with diversity is therefore a central condition of the lives of Indonesian Muslims, as John Bowen (2003) has shown in his study of how Muslims in Aceh Province work to reconcile Islamic laws, local customary laws, and secular state laws. The translations between these different legal regimes, Bowen suggests, show how people with deep differences in values can live together and create something that resembles the pluralism idealized by secular liberalism. In light of such observations, it is thus not surprising that many scholars have written about Indonesian Muslims practicing progressive politics, which, as I will elaborate in the following chapter, has contributed to Indonesia's image as a "good" Muslim country in the contemporary geopolitical context.[1]

At the same time, these long-standing conversations about coexistence amid diversity have become much more urgent in the post–New Order era. As previously discussed, democracy has enabled the emergence of multiple groups of Islamists. Radical Islamists use vigilantism and violence to implement sharia law (which they take to mean the suppression of vice, which includes the prohibition of the sale of alcohol, and the forced veiling of women), while moderate Islamists contest in the polls, secure seats in parliament, and enact legislative changes to widen Islam's political reach. These developments have led to concerns regarding growing intolerance and exclusivity in Indonesian society, prompting a redoubling of efforts to promulgate progressive interpretations of Islam, such as those undertaken by the youths in Formaci. The ability of young Indonesians to participate in the reconfiguration of Islam has been made possible by the recent rise of what some scholars call "pop religion," or forms of religiosity that have been mass mediated through the Internet, films, music, and other forms of popular culture that are targeted largely at young people (Weintraub 2011). An example, as discussed by Carla Jones (2007), is the proliferation of magazines and clothing stores that teach young Indonesian women how to be Muslim and fashionable at the same time. Importantly, pop religion allows young people to imagine themselves as important religious actors with the ability to create new forms of religious expressions.

The youthfulness of Formaci's enterprise can be observed in the important role of play—which is manifested in the form of humor, laughter, games, music, having fun, and saying dangerous things about Islam—in the work of religious interpretation. While there have been extensive analyses of play in relation to youth culture, the role of play in religion is relatively understudied. One exception is Asef Bayat's (2010) analysis of how Islamist political regimes in the Middle East try to control fun. Defining fun as ad hoc, nonroutine, and joyful conduct that enables people to break free from the constraints of life, Bayat argues that there was never a sweeping rejection of fun in Islamic history. Drinking, humor, music, dancing, and the enjoyment of food were widespread in medieval Islam, even though some groups were opposed to such activities. According to Bayat, systematic anti-fun attitudes appeared only in the 1980s as Islamist groups were seized by moral panic over youths adopting "sinful" and "alien" practices like dating, concerts, and movies. Fun began to be seen as threatening because it disrupts religious order and discipline. Instead of eradicating such practices, however, Islamist prohibitions merely drive it underground, as Muslim youths partake in such activities in secrecy. Pascal Menoret's study (2014) on the prevalence of joyriding in ultraconservative Saudi Arabia is one example of underground fun that offers a temporarily release from the boredom, lack of employment opportunities, and a shrinking space for personal freedom facing male Saudi youths.

Taking play to be a central element in religious improvisation, or how Muslims adapt their religion to a world where the values of secular liberalism have become hegemonic, this chapter explores the complicated relationship between play and religion and how play affects the interpretation of religious scriptures. On the one hand, play enables Indonesian youths to absorb the lessons of Western social sciences and humanities and subvert established religious beliefs and practices. On the other hand, when youths encounter resistance to their playful approach to religion, they present their efforts at religious reinterpretation as not antithetical to but aligned with the Islamic religious tradition. By subjecting play to religion, these youths are behaving like the subjects of Lara Deeb and Mona Harb's (2013) study on leisure—the Lebanese Muslims who must navigate the boom in cafés and restaurants in Beirut that cater to the young, fashionable, and pious. According to these authors, the decisions youths make to go to these establishments are not casual but in fact deeply ethical as they turn to their religious tradition to figure out, for example, what makes a café morally appropriate, and the circumstances allowing a Muslim to patronize an establishment that serves alcohol. By discussing the multiple dimensions of play in the religious lives of Indonesia's young liberals, I hope to illuminate the possibilities and limits of religious improvisation.

Self Study

My friends in the Indonesian civil society told me that if I wanted to understand student activism in the nation, I needed to conduct research in Formaci (the acronym for Forum Mahasiswa Ciputat, or the Ciputat Undergraduates Forum). Formaci started out as one of many reading groups at the State Islamic University but has become its most renowned. It was established in 1986 by three male students—Ihsan Ali-Fauzi, Saiful Mujani, and Budhy Munawar-Rahman—who wanted an informal venue to discuss how Islam could exist within a secular, development-oriented, and authoritarian political regime. The founders sought to welcome students from all backgrounds, and thus named the group in the most neutral way possible: after Ciputat, the district in which their university was located. Their decision to form a reading group was inspired by the first generation of leaders of independent Indonesia—such as President Sukarno, Vice President Hatta, and Prime Minister Syahrir—whose participation in student literary circles enabled them to develop anticolonialist ideas that came to define their subsequent political careers. Formaci is also an exemplar of this trend, with many of its affiliates, including the founders,

eventually carving out positions among Indonesia's most prominent public intellectuals and civil society activists.

The initial meeting with the students in Formaci was made possible
by my civil society friends who put us in touch. One telephone call explaining my research project was all it took to secure an invitation to the
group's headquarters, a rented house about a ten-minute walk from the
State Islamic University in a neighborhood replete with establishments
catering to undergraduates like bookstores, cafés, and photocopying facilities. The group's participants have diverse class, ethnic, and regional
backgrounds but share long-term exposure to Islamic education. Because
of a general blasé attitude toward formalities typically associated with
a student organization (there are, for instance, no recruitment drives or
binding membership rules), it is difficult to accurately quantify the total
number of participants in Formaci. Students interested in reading are welcome to join, with nothing preventing them from quitting if interest dis-
sipates. Nevertheless, it is clear that attendance numbers are small, about
the size of a seminar in an American academic setting. Nevertheless, as
I have stated previously, numerical minutiae should never be mistaken
for political insignificance. Formaci's participants are able to mobilize
popular support for liberal Islam on campus and beyond by organizing
mass-participation events like lectures, conferences, and film screenings.

Formaci's participants read texts broadly related to Islamic studies,
philosophy, and social sciences, categories that were determined by the
group's founders. While the syllabus varies annually, some books are read
so consistently by successive student cohorts that they are regarded as
part of the Formaci canon. These consist of a wide-ranging collection
of thinkers including progressive Muslim writers from Indonesia (Nurcholish Madjid, Ahmad Wahib) and abroad (Fazlur Rahman, Nasr Abu
Zayd), classical philosophers (Hegel, Heidegger), prominent Indonesian-
ists (Benedict Anderson, Clifford Geertz), classical sociologists (Karl
Marx, Max Weber), and contemporary sociologists and critical theorists
(Theodor Adorno, Pierre Bourdieu, Anthony Giddens, Max Horkheimer).
Each year, Formaci's participants add new books to the reading list based
on their assessment of pressing contemporary questions. In recent years,
for instance, neoliberalism has become such a buzzword in the Indonesian
political economy that students have appended books on this topic to
their syllabus. Texts written by non-Indonesian authors are usually read

in Indonesian translations, which are relatively easy to acquire thanks to a vibrant translating, publishing, and bookselling industry in the nation. The syllabus is planned collaboratively by the students at the beginning of each semester. Anyone can suggest book titles, authors, and topics, but ultimately the group must reach a consensus on whether they want to read those works. With no "grades" or "levels" in Formaci, all participants new and seasoned read the same books and discuss them in an integrated setting. "Official" discussions usually begin in the late afternoon and last for approximately two hours; impromptu discussions, however, can occur anytime.

Before I describe a typical Formaci meeting, I will offer a sketch of how scholars have theorized the act of reading. Within anthropology and neighboring disciplines, reading has been an important object of investigation for scholars studying "complex" (as opposed to "primitive") societies. While earlier scholars like Jack Goody (1968) examined how literacy allowed people to transcend their ethnic and spatial locations and develop universalist consciousness, more recent scholars focused on the cultural specificities of reading practices, insisting that there is no one way to read (e.g., Boyarin 1993). Scholars generally agree that there is a slippage between the meaning inscribed in a text by its author and the interpretation that its readers might make of the text. Michel de Certeau tells us that "whether it is a question of newspapers or Proust, the text has a meaning only through its readers; it changes along with them; it is ordered in accord with codes of perception it does not control" (1984, 170–71). The observation made by Certeau can certainly be applied to Islamic scriptures, which Muslims read but from which they take away different meanings. To understand variety in interpretation, it is also important to heed Roger Chartier's reminder that reading "is not uniquely an abstract operation of the intellect: it brings the body into play, it is inscribed in a space and a relationship with oneself or with others" (1994, 8). In other words, this chapter is not just a study of what liberals read, but also of the acquisition of embodied practices that are implicated in how they read.

At every meeting, Formaci's participants take turns assuming the role of a moderator or a presenter who summarizes the main arguments in the assigned text. During the first discussion I attended, there were eleven men and three women, all sitting on the floor of the living room without any separation between the sexes, some with outstretched legs and others cross-legged, most of them resting their backs against the walls. Some people had coffee in one hand, cigarette in the other. The topic of the day was "epistemology." The moderator, a senior undergraduate who had participated in Formaci since his freshman year, was responsible for directing the conversation such that each of the major themes in the reading materials (which were complex philosophical concepts like "rationality," "skepticism," and "the truth") gets discussed. Employing a broadly Socratic method, he called on people to ensure that everyone (including me) made an active contribution in dissecting the readings. It was evident, however, that some students were more vocal than others and exuded greater confidence. Such students were either majors in Islamic philosophy, or seasoned participants who had read the same materials in previous years, or had informally sought the assistance of Formaci's alumni members to understand the abstract concepts. Despite the knowledge disparity, no one acted as a pedagogical authority who had the final word on what the correct answers were. There were no loose ends to be tied, or conclusions to be reached; the point, it seemed, was to let everyone have a stab at interpreting the readings.

This pedagogy is different from how knowledge is conventionally attained in the madrasas where Formaci's participants receive their pre-university education. Madrasas offer a classical Islamic education that focuses on Quranic recitation for beginners and gradually includes other subjects as students advance, like Quranic exegesis, traditions of the Prophet, Islamic theology, and Arabic language. Madrasa education is concerned with the faithful transmission of an author's true message. The written text is treated with suspicion, not because Muslim educators did not value reading or writing, but because it is perceived as unable to convey the real intentions of its absent author. In order to understand a text's authentic meaning, the written word must be subjected to the superior authority of orality. The paradigm for this is how the Quran is studied: not by silent reading, but by reciting the verses and subsequently committing them to memory. But how is one to know that one is reciting and memorizing the text in the manner intended by the author? Where it is not possible to consult the author personally, one must learn from a scholar who can establish an intellectual genealogy to the author. "Between me and the author are two men," said a religious scholar in Brinkley Messick's study describing how he received the knowledge from a teacher, who in

turn received it from another individual who studied with the original author (1993, 15). In other words, the established ideal in Islamic education
is not to acquire knowledge independently, but through the teacher-to-
student mode of transmission.

Global developments since the turn of the twentieth century, however, have enabled Muslims to seek religious knowledge independently
of teachers. Widespread availability of religious texts as a result of mass
printing, as well as increases in literacy rates as a result of mass secular
schooling, meant that ordinary Muslims no longer needed to enroll in
seminaries to acquire knowledge of the Islamic sciences. New channels
of learning like independent reading became available and further multiplied with subsequent media innovations like cassette tapes, television,
and the Internet. Reading on their own allowed ordinary Muslims to experiment with ideas that may depart from religious orthodoxy. This intellectual ferment results in the rise of what many scholars call "modernist
Islam," whose proponents have not only self-consciously adopted modern
values (such as rationality, science, and constitutionalism) but also strive
to preserve and improve the Islamic faith in the modern world.[2] While
modernist Muslims vary tremendously in terms of their politics and religious views, they seek to challenge the exclusive purview that the religious
teacher has over religious interpretation. By expressing confidence in their
own qualifications—whether derived from madrasa education, modern
education, or personal virtuosity—they are able to declare themselves
"new religious authorities" (Eickelman and Anderson 1999).

Formaci should be seen as a continuation of this global trend that began
over a century ago. Thus, unlike in classical Islamic education, where rote
learning under the teacher's supervision predominates, the transmission of
religious interpretations in Formaci occurs through unstructured conversations like the one below. This is a reconstruction based on my field notes
of the discussion I attended, which tackled the topic of epistemology:

Moderator: Let's talk about certainty in knowledge. How can we know for
               certain that something is true? Any thoughts?
Participant 1: That's a tricky one. How can I have certainty that I am indeed hand-
               some and that he [*pointing to another male participant*] is hideous?
               Should I judge it based on what I see in the mirror? Or is it that I'm
               able to attract more girls than he can? [*laughter from group*]

Moderator [*turning to me*]:	What do you think, *Mas* [Mr.]?
Author [*tentatively*]:	Certainty in knowledge is an important issue, but sorry, I can't really discuss it in an abstract philosophical way. I tend to approach the question in an empirical, positivist manner. For example, my research looks at the socialization of both liberal and Islamist youths. So I have to collect information that allows me to observe how they become liberals or Islamists.
Participant 2:	Well, you can compare their beliefs. Islamists believe that Islam controls all parts of your life. We [liberals] don't. We believe in religious freedom.
Participant 3:	But what is religious freedom? How can we define it?
Participant 1:	Islam recognizes religious freedom. For example, look at the Al Kafirun chapter of the Quran, verse 6. [*Begins reciting*] "Say: 'O unbelievers! I do not worship what you worship, Nor do you worship what I worship, Nor will I ever worship what you worship, Nor will you ever worship what I worship. You have your religion, And I have mine.'"
Participant 4:	But doesn't the Quran also oppose religious freedom? Just look at the Al Imran chapter, verse 19. "Whoso blasphemes against God's revelations, God is swift in reckoning."
Moderator:	But why do we have to look to Islam? UUD 1945 [the Indonesian constitution] guarantees religious freedom. We should just go by what the constitution says.

"But why do we have to look to Islam?" is precisely the type of antiauthority question that students are allowed to ask within Formaci's self-study setting, where students can read texts without being led to prescribed intellectual or religious ends. Although they were undergraduates in pursuit of a bachelor's degree, some participants told me that their "real education" occurred in the reading circle rather than the classrooms of the Islamic university. One such student would go to classes for the purpose of debating with his professors and classmates so he could show off the knowledge attained in Formaci; another had neglected his classes to the extent that he was getting credit for an average of only one course per semester. Such attitudes account for why even the most widely read and articulate participants in Formaci were at best mediocre performers in the university. When I inquired about their seeming apathy toward coursework, the students explained that what they were rejecting were the constraints posed by the didactic classroom setting. First, not all professors had progressive politics, and rarely were they tolerant of anything resembling religious critique. Second, even the progressive professors would impose limits in class discussions, asking students to not say overly disrespectful things toward Islam so as not to offend other people's religious convictions. Censorship barriers or norms of politeness encountered in the classrooms were absent in Formaci, thus allowing the most heterodox and improvisational behaviors to be unleashed.

Madrasas and the Possibility of Critique

While the Formaci discussions approach texts differently from how they would be treated in classical Islamic education, the seeds for the participants' critical stance toward religion have actually been sown during their time in the madrasa. In other words, my claim is that their progressive politics developed because of—rather than despite of—madrasa education. This argument might seem counterintuitive. After all, the pedagogical salience of recitation and memorization has led to enduring stereotypes that Islamic education negates any form of thinking. This stereotype seemed to be affirmed with the rise of Islamic radicalism. In 1996, when Kabul fell under the control of Taliban fighters educated in Afghan and Pakistani madrasas, Islamic schools were portrayed in the West as backward-looking institutions devoted to the brainwashing of young Muslims. Furthermore, there is a powerful assumption that critique, or the ability to unveil error, is associated with rational deliberation rather than religious thought. As observed by Wendy Brown, many secular liberals believe that "the true, the objective, the real, the rational, and even the scientific emerge only with the shedding of religious authority or 'prejudice.' . . . [Hence] the conviction that critique replaces opinion or faith with truth, and subjectivism with science; that critique is, in short, secular" (2009, 11). Yet anthropological and historical accounts from various cross-cultural contexts have portrayed Islamic schools as active and re-flexive participants in public debates, hardly the bastions of unthinking they are often made out to be.[3]

To make the case that critique can be fostered by religion, I will start by offering a snapshot of madrasa education in Indonesia. With some forty-seven thousand of them in the nation, madrasas are deeply hetero-geneous. Some key variations include the following:

(a) Degree of modernization: Over the past century, Muslim educators have argued vigorously over whether Islamic education should retain its traditional character or emulate Western education, for example by introducing the separation of age-grades, examinations, and secu-lar subjects. Thus some schools teach a traditional Islamic curriculum, while others offer a modern curriculum consisting of Islamic and sec-ular subjects.

(b) Religious orientation: Some schools are known for promoting conser-vative social attitudes—for example, that men are superior to women, that Islam is the only true religion, and that things associated with the West (ranging from denim trousers to television and secular democ-racy) should be treated with disdain. Other schools are influenced by the teachings of the progressive religious leader and fourth Indonesian president, Abdurrahman Wahid (1999–2001), which means that stu-dents are taught that democracy, interfaith tolerance, and pluralism are supported by Islam. It should be noted that a school's religious ori-entation does not correlate with its degree of modernization.

When I examined the type of madrasas where the young liberals in Formaci were educated, I discovered that, surprisingly, they emerged from both traditional schools and modern schools, both progressive schools and conservative schools. This finding undermined my assumption that most of them would have graduated from modern and progressive ma-drasas. How is it possible that liberals could emerge from seemingly any-where in the network of Islamic schools? One explanation is specific to Indonesia. The Indonesian government has continually sought to integrate madrasas into the national education system via a number of initiatives: for instance, ensuring that Islamic schools teach secular subjects using the same textbooks as secular schools, and making Islamic schools participate in the national policy of compulsory nine years of education. Robert Hefner (2009) argues that these policies had the overall impact of aligning Islamic schools with the multiethnic and multireligious principles of Indonesian nationalism, even though there were educators who maintained a conservative religious outlook. A second explanation pertains to the features of Islamic education more generally. Instead of stifling critical thinking, Islamic education actually encourages deliberation and debate among students—essential ingredients in the formation of liberal Muslims. I will point to two such features in the madrasa curriculum, though by no means should this be regarded as an exhaustive list.

First is the study of *fiqh* or Islamic jurisprudence, the foundational subject of religious education. Fiqh is an Islamic science concerned with elaborating how God's commandments in the Quran can be applied to everyday life in matters ranging from worship to etiquette, marriage, crime, statehood, and commercial transactions. The primary type of manual used in fiqh lessons is the *matan* (Arabic, root meaning is "text"). These are authoritative manuals written by classical jurists that specify the proper codes of conduct pertaining to the various life domains mentioned above. The prose in the matan is terse and in rhyme (that is, nonmetrical rhymed prose), composed as such in order to aid memorization. But the abbreviated prose often renders the matan incomprehensible on its own and needing to be studied alongside supplementary texts called *sharh* (commentaries) and *hashiya* (summaries).[4] The relationship between the matan and these supplementary texts can be described using a botanical analogy: if the matan is a tree trunk, then the commentaries and summaries are the many branches that sprout from it. In other words, the matan is an unchanged paradigmatic text that invites numerous and often conflicting attempts by jurists who seek to clarify and elucidate its meanings. In this multiplicity lies the potential instability of authoritative texts. While each madrasa teacher will privilege a particular branch of the matan, the fragmented character of Islamic knowledge means that no arguments could be made conclusively.

This brings me to the second feature that encourages critical thinking: the vital place that self-study occupies in the educational system. Self-study is often overlooked in accounts of Islamic pedagogy because this is a culture of knowledge that privileges the teacher-to-student mode of transmission. Yet ethnographic accounts from madrasas in Indonesia,

Morocco, and Yemen indicate that students actually spend long hours studying without their teachers.[5] Self-study can take the form of peer learning (studying with contemporaries) or autodidactic learning (studying by oneself). Whereas formal lessons are devoted to the memorization and consumption of texts following the teacher's dictates, self-study presents an opportunity for students to bypass this pedagogical script. It is this freedom that allowed the Indonesian students in Zamakhsyari Dhofier's work ([1982] 1999) to explore branches of jurisprudential interpretation not taught by their teachers, or the Moroccan students in Dale Eickelman's work (1978) to read literature from outside the religious curriculum. I am not suggesting that students will always undermine their teachers; after all, the Islamic educational system strives for coherence in its reproduction of authoritative religious views. What I am saying is that because the Islamic educational system is not a hermetic discursive space, students who disagree with their teachers can seek recourse in alternative interpretations.

In short, there are important features in madrasa education that promote the ability of students to analyze and evaluate information to reach a conclusion. This explains why liberal Muslims could emerge from conservative and traditional schools. One example was Lulu, who was in her late thirties and a participant in Formaci in the 1990s. When we met during my research, Lulu was making a name for herself as an up-and-coming feminist in Jakarta and was a senior to Formaci's existing participants. Before entering university, Lulu was schooled in a conservative madrasa where teachers espoused the notion that women were inferior and willful beings who needed men's supervision. She found these antiwomen jurisprudential views to be incongruous with the empirical realities of her life. Lulu's grandmother, who had established a coeducational school in a small town in Banten Province, was a respected community leader as well as a feared headmaster—a person Lulu could not fathom being regarded as weak or inferior. Lulu's disagreements with her teachers were also shaped by another important factor. She was the owner of a large collection of novels from an early age, thanks to a doting father who regularly purchased them for her soon after their publication. Reading by herself, she said, endowed her with a fertile imagination, which was why she was profoundly unsettled by the "poverty of ideas" (*kemiskinan ide*) presented by her teachers.

Another example was Firdaus. Educated in a conservative madrasa with a decently stocked library, Firdaus was appointed head student librarian, a position that allowed him to read widely. He took to heart the advice given by one of his teachers: "Young man, do not be allergic to books. Read whatever books you can find because each one of them will be useful to you. I despise Marx and Nietzsche, but I still read their books because I can learn something from them." For his teacher, the purpose of reading works by thinkers like Marx or Nietzsche was to "defeat their arguments" (*menghancurkan argumennya*)—in other words, to find weaknesses in their theoretical concepts in order to affirm the veracity of Islam's teachings. Firdaus, however, developed a different attitude. Spending time among the library's stacks allowed him to discover the writings of liberal Muslim thinkers, which he found attractive because their version of religion was tolerant and not based on an a priori rejection of non-Muslim cultures. The dissatisfaction he felt with some aspects of his religious education led him to participate in Formaci—which is well known in madrasa communities as a gathering of intelligent people—once he enrolled in the State Islamic University.

Whereas madrasa education created a potential for transforming people like Lulu and Firdaus into liberal Muslims, it is university education that allowed for the potential to be fulfilled. In recent years, the state Islamic university system in Indonesia has received accolades in the Muslim world for its efforts to breach the separation between Islamic and secular branches of knowledge. As discussed previously, these efforts began during the New Order, to diminish tension between Muslims and secular modernity. State Islamic universities incorporated Western scholarly approaches to the study of Islam in the 1970s–1980s, thus exposing undergraduates to the historicizing perspectives offered by courses like anthropology, sociology, and philosophy. This was facilitated by the recruitment of young Indonesian lecturers who had pursued graduate degrees in Islamic studies in universities like McGill, Leiden, Chicago, Columbia, and Ohio State. Many of these lecturers combined the new approaches to the study of Islam with liberal social attitudes on issues like democratization, religious pluralism, and women's rights. The curricular reforms inspired student activists to establish reading circles like Formaci to discuss alternative ways of thinking about religion.

Several factors influenced the decision by these activists to call themselves "liberal." One source of inspiration was a collection of essays by progressive Muslims from across the globe compiled by the American sociologist Charles Kurzman (1998) in a book titled *Liberal Islam*, thus demonstrating the feedback loop that academic works can generate. The term had also been used by the reformist thinker Nurcholish Madjid in a 1970 speech that is now considered a founding moment in the liberal Islam movement. Madjid's landmark speech, titled "The Urgency of Religious Renewal and the Problem of Integration in the Muslim Community," addressed the obsolescence and fossilization of religious beliefs that have stymied Islam's dynamism (*obsolete memfosil, kehilangan dinamika*). To overcome this malaise, Madjid argued for the practice of a liberal Islam (*Islam yang liberal*) that protects intellectual freedom and the freedom of religious expressions. A central feature of this religious model is "secularization," a term that Madjid used in a very particular way to refer to the ability to distinguish religious practices that are sacred, transcendental, and divinely ordained from those that are temporal, context dependent, and humanly created. The implication is that the latter can be altered to suit evolving historical circumstances, thus allowing Islam to be more receptive to the ever-changing needs of its adherents.[6]

Adopting "liberal" to denote progressive religiosity meant that liberal Muslims had to confront the excess of meaning the term brings. The word itself is long controversial in Indonesia. While liberal democracy was implemented in 1950 shortly after independence, President Sukarno eventually denounced it for promoting conflict (supposedly a feature of "the West") rather than harmony (which was "Indonesian"). This became the justification for Sukarno's implementation in 1957 of "guided democracy" (*demokrasi terpimpin*), a consensus-based system modeled after the guardianship of village elders and which sought to establish power-sharing between secular nationalist, Muslim, and Communist factions. It is possible that Sukarno's policies set a local precedence for marking "liberal" as signifying dissent and disunity, which is why liberal Muslims are often accused of destroying Islam. Fearing that the controversies surrounding "liberal" would distract people from the movement's aims, some liberals proposed alternative labels like *pluralis, progresif, demokratis*, or *emancipatoris*. Yet most supported the continued use of "liberal" precisely because its scandalous character helped generate publicity for the movement. Some liberal Muslims subsequently pushed for a comprehensive theorization of the relationship between liberal Islam and Western conceptions of political and economic liberalism. The liberal Muslims I know, however, were uninterested in this project, preferring to restrict their activism to the promotion of progressive reinterpretations of Islamic scriptures.

Humorous Muslims

Will Muslims develop progressive politics if they consume the Western human sciences? Rizal certainly thought so. "We in Formaci don't read the Quran or the hadiths or other classical texts," he said, describing the group's pedagogy. "Instead, we study religion historically and sociologically—how religions arise, the functions of religion, why religions attract people, why religions fail. Muslims are taught to look at Islam as the perfect religion, which is why they never criticize it. But in Formaci, we learn to look at it contextually, like an analyst. So we talk about the problems in the religion." While Western academic texts may have shaped the religious and political outlook of Rizal and his contemporaries, it is important to note that these texts do not have a similarly transformative impact on the many other Muslims who read them, perhaps most famously the erudite ayatollahs of Iran.[7] As I have stated previously, interpretations of texts are heavily contingent on a moral universe that valorizes particular types of reception. It is thus important that we investigate the contextual factors allowing the Western academic texts to influence liberal Muslims in contemporary Indonesia the way they do.

One important factor is the enlarged space for humor in the post-Suharto political discourse. Humor is a potent weapon of critique. Observing the important role of visual humor and veiled satire in the traditional shadow puppet theater known as *wayang kulit*, Benedict Anderson suggests that satirical art is very old in Indonesia (1990, 67). During the New Order, however, Suharto's aversion to political humor and the constraints he placed on media freedom led to the decline of satire in public arenas, as seen, for instance, in the dwindling publication and sales of comic art in the 1980s–1990s, despite robustness in preceding decades (Lent 2015). Satire made a comeback during the post–New Order, as evidenced by the groundbreaking television show *Republik Mimpi* (Republic of Dreams) that was launched in 2005 and which opened the floodgates for other satirical programs.[8] Inspired by the popular American satirist Jon Stewart, the show features a panel of comedians who play top politicians. One character, an engineer singularly obsessed with turning Indonesia into a technological giant, is based on B. J. Habibie, president of the transitional government in 1998–1999. Another character, who sleeps throughout the show, is based on Abdurrahman Wahid, president in 1999–2001, who was notorious for dozing off during meetings. Satire's recent comeback signals to Indonesians that it is acceptable to mock power, which is perhaps why political leaders today are consistently subject to humorous skewering in Indonesian cyberspace.[9]

When discussing humor and politics in Indonesia, it is important to acknowledge the legacy of Abdurrahman Wahid. Before becoming president, Wahid was a top religious cleric who helmed Nahdlatul Ulama, an organization that claims more than fifty million members and administers many religious services in the nation, including education. While Nahdlatul Ulama's base remains deeply traditionalist and conservative, Wahid was progressive. As a student in Cairo's Al Azhar University in the 1960s, for example, he notably rebelled against the traditionalism of its faculty by refusing to learn more scriptures, and instead studied Marxism, read English and French books, watched New Wave films, and eventually transferred elsewhere.[10] Wahid also liked to joke.[11] One memorable story I read online, though quite possibly apocryphal, was that Wahid made Saudi Arabia's sullen King Fahd laugh so loud that he showed his gums publicly for the first time. Wahid's signature colloquial Indonesian saying, "Gitu aja kok repot," which is perhaps best translated as "Don't sweat the small stuff," encapsulates the easygoing attitude found in his humor. Predictions that Wahid's wit and the message of reconciliation that he preached would help to unite a divided nation, however, proved to be incorrect when Wahid was impeached in 2001, after just twenty-one months in office, on charges of corruption and incompetence.

In contrast to his short-lived presidency, Wahid's humor has had a more lasting impact on the conduct of public debate, particularly on religion. Indonesians tell me that Wahid's humor is typical of the Islamic educational environment. They associate it most closely with Islamic boarding schools (which Indonesians call *pesantren*), where students eat, sleep, study, and live in close quarters for extended periods, which means that humor plays an important function in alleviating boredom as well as ensuring a harmonious coexistence. Additionally, many Indonesians regard humor as compatible with the openness of the religious curriculum I described earlier. Perhaps this is why "*santri* humor" (or the humor of *pesantren* students) is such a popular genre in Indonesian bookstores. Regardless of whether Wahid's joking manner traces a genealogy to Islamic education, it is clear that religiously educated liberals view Wahid as a role model. "Gus Dur," said Rizal, referring to Wahid by his nickname, "shows us that religion doesn't have to be so serious all the time," implying that the jokes, mischief, pranks, music, and poetry that intersperse Formaci's intellectual activities are not only a marker of youthfulness, but could also be seen as Wahidian.

In the West there is a pervasive stereotype of Muslims as humorless, as evidenced in popular commentaries regarding how Muslims overwhelmingly rejected the satirical depictions of the Prophet Muhammad in the Danish newspaper *Jyllands-Posten* in 2005 and the French magazine *Charlie Hebdo* in 2015. As Don Kulick (2010) has argued, the portrayal of an entire group of people as lacking humor has the effect of denying them their humanity, thus making it easier for society to denigrate or eliminate them completely. Obviously Muslims, like other people, have a sense of humor. In recent years, Muslims have also begun to deploy humor for political purposes, in part because they are learning from the satirical activism associated with prominent television personalities like Jon Stewart and Stephen Colbert. The documentary *The Muslims Are Coming!*, for example, showcases American Muslim comedians who tour middle America to make white audiences laugh and challenge the stereotype of the angry Muslims (Farsad and Obeidallah 2013). Across the Middle East, Muslim comics have begun to create media targeted at Muslim audiences in which they portray ISIS jihadists as bumbling fools in order to delegitimize the group's claim as Muslim authority. Humor, in other words, becomes a counterterrorism measure.

In Formaci, humor plays an important role in the acquisition of knowledge. One observation I made was how participants often resorted to humor when engaging in discussions about complex theories. My earlier description of the "epistemology" meeting, where one discussant tries to explain the weighty concept of "truth" by referencing his good looks compared to another person's seemingly unattractive features, is a typical instance, employing lowbrow insults on other people's physical appearances, be it chubbiness, thinness, unkemptness, crooked teeth, or dark skin. Unsurprisingly, men are typically the perpetrators and victims of such jokes. Compared to women, men spend more time in the house and hence develop the easy rapport that allows them to identify and poke fun at one another's physical shortcomings. Another type of humor jokes with intellectual concepts, for instance, when someone who is nosy is told, "Don't be such a panopticon," in reference to Michel Foucault's discussion of the modern prison. Humor might be introduced to the discussions simply to make them more fun, but it appears to have other important consequences. Rizal told me that complex theories by great thinkers can become less intimidating and more accessible when ridiculed or discussed in a lighthearted manner. This offers some measure of comfort, especially for new participants, many of whom have little prior acquaintance with Western social sciences and humanities and face great difficulty in understanding them.

Formaci's participants also liked to make religion the target of jokes. Once, during a conversation, a student posed this riddle to me: "What is the name of the devil?" "Toni," was the answer. "Why Toni?" I asked. He then recited: "Audhu billahi min al-shai*Ton Ir*-rajim" (I seek refuge with Allah from the accursed Satan), manipulating the incantation that Muslims usually recite to form "the devil's name." Another student once wrote his status update on Facebook in a way that parodied the tone in which a Quranic injunction would be written: "O Facebookers! Fill your status updates with good news rather than sighs and complaints. Truly, your friends prefer people with a positive outlook." Examples of more intensely provocative religious humor will be mentioned later, but here I would like to point out that there is a prevailing attitude in Formaci that nothing is so transcendent that it cannot be lampooned. Making fun of religion subverts the orthodox view that religion should be treated reverentially, and such humor certainly ventures beyond the type associated with Abdurrahman Wahid. Indeed, such jokes can invite treacherous consequences when made in "real" life, as not only does Indonesia have a blasphemy law that criminalizes antireligious acts, but Islamist vigilante groups are often quick to assault individuals and groups perceived as heretical. In Formaci's mischievous self-study setting, however, such forms of humor are not only tolerated but also encouraged. Participants, especially the newer ones, who express discomfort with the religious mockery will themselves be teased.

By making fun of complex theories and religion, Formaci's participants appear to have concocted a recipe for a change in mind-set as to how they view religion. Rizal's experiences were fairly typical. In an interview about the early stages of his involvement with the group, he recounted how deeply troubled he was by the academic books he read. What bothered him was not that their theoretical approaches departed from classical religious education, but that he found their arguments convincing. He regarded the atheistic existentialism of Nietzsche and Sartre as especially nightmarish because he could not disagree with its fundamental principles—that there is no empirical evidence for the existence of God. Finding his faith challenged, Rizal nearly quit the group. He stayed only when more seasoned participants, who had gone through similar struggles, persuaded him to persist in spite of his personal turmoil. It was only much later, when he discovered more scholarly approaches to religion beyond existentialism, that he began to feel at ease in Formaci. "I found myself no longer interested in discussing whether God existed or not, because both sides of the argument cannot provide empirical proof. So whether you want to believe in God or not, that's your choice. But whether God exists or not, the fact is religion is everywhere. So I think it's better to talk about something concrete, like the effects of religion on life. I suppose I became more influenced by sociologists like Émile Durkheim and Peter Berger."

Anthropologists of religion would say that the changes in Rizal's religious beliefs should be seen not simply as a phenomenon of the interior, but as occurring through the power of bodily habit. Rejecting the notion of piety as innate, Saba Mahmood (2005) argues that Muslims become pious by subjecting themselves to religion and aligning the conduct of their everyday lives with religious tenets. As previously noted, however, Mahmood's research subjects are conservative Islamists, which means that their religious socialization cannot stand for all Muslims. In fact, the formation of liberal Muslims seems to entail an embodied process that is the opposite of what Mahmood described. Instead of their acting piously, there appears to be a divestment or abandonment of pious acts among liberals. Although Formaci's participants have been socialized in the madrasa to the punctilious performance of religious rituals, nearly all of them eventually stop praying or fasting after joining the group. "I was praying five times each day when I joined Formaci," said a student. "Then it became four, three, two, one. And I can tell you the exact date I stopped praying altogether." Another student suggested that there was a dialectical relationship between his impiety and the consumption of the Formaci literature: the more convincing the books became, the less he prayed; the less he prayed, the more convincing the books became. When I asked why that was the case, his response was rhetorical. "Would you feel like praying if you kept reading books telling you that religion is a social construct?"

Yet another student went beyond his own impiety and took devious pleasure in expressing antireligious views for the sake of rattling others. During a meeting, he questioned whether the Prophet Muhammad should be seen as a moral exemplar. Why did the prophet have eleven wives when other men were allowed four? Was the Prophet a pedophile for marrying Aisha when she was just nine years old? Was he being anti-Semitic when he persecuted his Jewish enemies? Given that these issues have been amply discussed among Muslims, a few people in the group started to offer answers that justify why the Prophet did what he did in each of those instances. His multiple marriages were necessary for building political alliances for securing Islam's existence, said one person. In medieval Near Eastern societies, girls who have reached puberty were regarded as adults who could get married, said another person. Muhammad punished the Jews for breaking a political alliance and hence committing treason, not for their religious beliefs, said yet another person. "Ah! This is all nonsense! Why do you all keep believing Muhammad's lies?" the provocative young man said scornfully. "You're so *norak* [tasteless or tawdry]!" someone shouted. "Well, I'm just trying to get you to reflect on why you believe what you believe," he retorted. Seeing that people were still riled up, he laughed and laughed.[12]

The Possibilities and Limits of Religious Improvisation

Play transforms Formaci's participants. Not only do they speak about religion using a secular liberal lexicon; they also insist that religion has to be dissected and subject to reason and critical analysis. This is evident in Rizal's reflection on how he has changed since being a member of the study circle. "When I was in the madrasa, I took a literal approach to the Quran. But this is not rational [*rasional*], because the meaning is derived literally, without understanding the context for why the verse was revealed. In Formaci, I learned that it is very important for us to be able to legitimize [*melegitimasikan*] our religious beliefs and actions using logical thinking [*berfikir secara logis*] rather than basing them on assumptions." As student activists, Rizal and his peers are eager to apply their liberal interpretation of religion by participating in public conversations about what it means to be Muslim in democratic Indonesia. During my field-work, I noted several instances of their efforts, including working with liberal Muslim NGOs to publish literature on religious freedom, organiz-ing a public lecture on campus on the rights of sexual minorities featuring a notable gay author and activist, and taking part in protests against gov-ernment policies that restrict civil rights (for example, the previously dis-cussed Antipornography Bill).

Formaci's participants interact regularly with their seniors, who give them advice about the possibilities and limits of religiously improvisa-tional behavior. Guided by nostalgia for their student days and a sense of obligation toward their juniors, the seniors make it a point to keep abreast of developments in Formaci, sometimes by showing up at group discussions or inviting the students out for a meal. Many seniors also attend the annual meeting where Formaci elects its own group leaders, an event cheekily named "the papal conclave" (*konsili*). Persons who are hardworking, intelligent, and demonstrate competency over the reading materials will be elected by their peers to be officeholders. Depending on the group's need for the year, sometimes one person is elected leader, while at other times three or four people will share the responsibility. When a sole person is appointed, he or she will be called the "imam" (while Islamic orthodoxy forbids women from being imam in a mixed-gender setting, Formaci has subverted convention by electing female imams over the years). When a group of persons is chosen as co-leaders, they will be known rather grandiosely as the "presidium." During the elections, the seniors take the opportunity to discuss the state of the liberal Islam move-ment with the students, as well as talent-scout for new blood to join the NGOs where they work.

One of the seniors, Zainal, cautions the students that making liberal arguments about religion can be very dangerous business. He speaks from experience. In June 2008, for example, he joined other participants from the National Alliance for the Freedom of Religion and Faith,[13] a loose coalition of pro-democracy activists and liberal Muslims, in a show of solidarity for a Muslim sect called the Ahmadiyah. While the majority of Muslims believe that the Prophet Muhammad was God's final messenger, the followers of Ahmadiyah believe that Muhammad was succeeded by the sect's founder, Mirza Ghulam Ahmad (d. 1908). Its divergence from Islamic orthodoxy meant that sect members have been barred by the government from proselytizing and subjected to condemnatory fatwa from authoritative Muslim organizations. The activists rallying for the Ahmadiyah condemn the ongoing persecution of the group, arguing that the Indonesian constitution guarantees religious freedom. Armed members of the Islamic Defenders Front, a hard-line group that has repeatedly inflicted bloody violence on the Ahmadiyah, arrived on the scene of the rally and grievously injured about seventy activists. For orchestrating the assault, the Islamic Defenders Front's leader, Rizieq Shibab, was sentenced to eighteen months in prison, a punishment that the victims regard as no more than a slap on the wrist.

In light of such incidents, mentors like Zainal repeatedly emphasize to the students that in order for liberal Muslim arguments to be persuasive with other Muslims, they must be grounded in Islamic scriptures as much as possible. Even though the students were influenced by thinkers like Hegel, Marx, and Foucault and subscribed to secular liberal ideals like democracy, human rights, and gender equality, they must formulate their reasoning based on the Quran, the hadiths, and Islamic jurisprudence. In other words, they should mirror the methodology employed by internationally prominent progressive Muslims like Khaled Abou el Fadl, Amina Wadud, and Fazlur Rahman. The advice of the mentors is historically sound, given that, as Talal Asad has observed, Muslims who have sought to change orthodox discourse have always worked within the confines of the Islamic religious tradition: "What is involved in such changes is not a simple ad hoc acceptance of new arrangements but the attempt to redescribe norms and concepts with the aid of tradition-guided reasoning. The authority of that redescription . . . has depended historically on how successful the underlying reasoning was judged to be" (1993, 211). The implication for Formaci's students is that even though they have evolved from their earlier days in a religious educational setting, they must retrieve the knowledge acquired from the madrasa in order to form their liberal Muslim arguments.

Let me describe an example. Previously, I discussed how Formaci's participants took part in a protest against their campus administration's decision to make head scarfs compulsory for female students. They believe that the policy contravened religious freedom, an important liberal principle, but they turn to the Quran to make their arguments. The starting point for these students, as it is for Muslims who argue that head scarfs are obligatory, is the following verse: "O Prophet, tell your wives, your daughters and women believers to wrap their outer garments closely around them, for this makes it more likely that they will be recognized and not be harassed. God is All-Forgiving, Compassionate to each."[14] The students argued that the verse should be understood in relation to seventh-century Arabia, where it was revealed. Prior to Islam's arrival, the students said, patriarchal Arabian society accorded a low status to women. Women who wore clothing exposing part of their bosoms were vulnerable to sexual assault by men, who students suggested had high libidos because of a diet composed primarily of meat. From this perspective, the Quran's injunction that women wear a garment that concealed their hair, neck, and chest was actually a means of protecting women from men's predatory behavior. The head scarf was meant to signify that women had dignity and must be treated with respect. It was a culturally appropriate item for the job, because Arab men and women were already familiar with head coverings, which they wore to shield themselves from the desert climate.

At the same time, the students added, the Quran did not place the responsibility for managing desires and keeping modesty solely on women. They cited another verse where God stated that the responsibility fell on both sexes: "Tell believing men to avert their eyes, and safeguard their private parts; this is more decent for them, and God is All-Experienced with what they do. Tell believing women to avert their eyes, and safeguard their private parts, and not to expose their attractions except what is visible."[15] They then claimed that Muslims who cite this verse tend to focus on its latter portion that addresses women, and neglect its command to men. When taken in their proper context, these verses should not be seen as law decreeing women to wear the head scarf. The head scarf happens to be a specific solution that was suitable for Arabian society. Rather, the universal principle of these verses touches on the importance of modesty, dignity, personal safety, and the ability to control base desires. It is not necessary for women to wear the head scarf so long as there are other mechanisms that can uphold these values. Drawing on Islamic jurisprudence, the students suggested that the head scarf should not be seen as *daruriyyah* (necessities), the neglect of which could lead to heresy. Rather, the head scarf is *tahsiniyyah* (beautification), a practice that pertains to the ethics of particular cultures. The head scarf is therefore not an obligation, implying that women should be free to decide whether or not they want to wear it.

Even when liberal Muslims capitulate to the Islamic scriptures, there is no guarantee that their arguments will be persuasive. Evidence from various cross-cultural contexts suggest that the sophisticated methodology of Muslim progressives and the complexity of their arguments may appeal to a small, educated portion of the population but often cause anger and confusion to others. They are, as Carool Kersten (2011) points out, cosmopolitans to few and heretics to many. In the case of Formaci's arguments against the head scarf policy, however, we will never know if people take such arguments as religiously authoritative. As I described in an earlier chapter, their invocation of tradition was overshadowed by a young man in the rally who uttered the kind of dangerous words that could only be said in Formaci's private play setting—"If this policy represents the true face of Islam, if this is a religion that forces people to do things against their will, then today I declare myself to be out of Islam!"— words that led to Formaci's participants being branded as heretical and threatened with violence. Play might enable these youths to acquire new secular liberal idioms, but it seems that in order to communicate these ideas to others, play must be disciplined.

5

FROM MODERATE INDONESIA
TO INDONISTAN

It is election season at the State Islamic University. Liberal Muslim students are campaigning hard to get their candidates elected to the student senate, the central governing body for students, which has traditionally set the tone for activism on university campuses. During the ban on student activism imposed by the New Order, student senators were carefully selected by the university administration. These days, however, student organizations nominate their own candidates, who, similar to national politicians, strew their publicity materials across the campus and the residential areas nearby and go from classroom to classroom to pitch their campaigns. Each successive year sees decisive victories by liberal Muslim student organizations, ensuring that the student senate remains under a liberal Muslim stranglehold. Despite the unbroken winning streak, they are fretting about a possible surprise victory by their Islamist rivals and decide to redouble their efforts to win the popular vote. Some are reaching out more aggressively to undecided voters; perhaps leaving no stone unturned, one candidate even sought supernatural intervention by sprinkling grains of uncooked rice blessed by supplications around the polling station. "We can't let the fundamentalists win," a liberal Muslim candidate says contemptuously of the Islamists. "They will destroy this university."

Liberal Muslim concerns about a conservative takeover extend beyond the confines of the university. Many Indonesians are genuinely worried about the growing influence of Islamists in their nation. They are alarmed that in Aceh, the morality police are forcing women to wear the hijab and arresting unmarried couples out on dates, while in the Jakarta metropolitan area, Islamist vigilantes are harassing religious minorities. In their publications and lectures, members of the older generation of Indonesian social activists have adopted the phrase "creeping shariatization" to describe such incidents, a phrase meant to highlight the sinister aspects of the formal implementation of sharia law. Those of the younger generation have also invented their own expression. When they heard news suggesting an Islamist advance, they would sometimes sigh and wonder aloud, "Is Indonesia turning into Indonistan?" At other times, they might react to these stories with an angry assertion, "This is Indonesia, not Indonistan!" "What do you mean 'Indonesia is not Indonistan'?" I asked some of these youths. "We're not Afghanistan or Pakistan where the sharia law is implemented," they would reply. "We're a moderate Muslim nation."

Since the al-Qaeda hijackers flew airplanes into New York City's twin towers on 9/11, Muslims across the globe have been clamoring to define themselves as "moderate" and condemn acts of violence committed in their names. The emergence of the label could be traced to the aftermath of the attacks as the administration of George W. Bush sought to distinguish between "good" and "bad" Muslims, identities that would be measured in relation to American liberal principles. Bad Muslims were not only synonymous with terrorism, but also responsible for gender-based oppression, the exclusion of minorities, and the lack of development. Good or moderate Muslims, on the other hand, desired a peaceful, civic coexistence, believed in democratic principles, and supported "us" in the war against "them." According to Mahmood Mamdani, these labels indicate that unless proven to be "good," every Muslim was presumed to be "bad" (2004, 15). In other words, unlike the legal maxim innocent until proven guilty, Muslims were regarded as guilty until proven innocent. This was in fact the guiding principle behind the post-9/11 detention of Muslims at Guantánamo Bay, in prisons in Iraq and Afghanistan, and at "black site" prisons in secret locations, often without ever having their guilt or innocence legally established. As Muslims were increasingly viewed through the security lens, they came under obligation to prove their innocence by joining in a war against bad Muslims.

To create moderate Muslims in the wake of 9/11, the United States (and other Western democracies) have sought to teach Muslims about good religion. A central thrust of this project is to educate Muslims about religious freedom, one of the fundamental rights in a democratic society, which stipulates that adherence to Islam should not be enforced by government and that there should not be discrimination against minorities.[1] Winnifred Sullivan observes that "Americans who may be able to agree on little else agree that religious freedom is one of the shining achievements of the United States, one that they are anxious to export around the world" (2005, 1). More concretely, the desire to export religious freedom has resulted in the swift expansion of an academic publishing industry on religion, as well as the proliferation of new government bodies that spearhead religious reform projects. Agencies for religious engagement have been established under the aegis of the departments of State and Homeland Security, the military, and USAID. By singling out religion as a basis for making foreign policy decisions, the United States has ushered in what Elizabeth Hurd (2015) calls "the new politics of religion," which displaces older practices of secularism where religion was conceived as private and largely irrelevant to global governance.

Projects to promote religious freedom have been carried out in full force in post–New Order Indonesia. They are spearheaded by civil society groups that have sprouted in the democratic era like mushrooms after a rainy day, from groups like KAPAL Perempuan that advocate for women's education and empowerment, to those like the Wahid Institute that advance the progressive legacy of Abdurrahman Wahid, or those like Freedom Institute that promote wide-ranging freedoms in religion, politics, and the economy. If you attend the public advocacy events organized by these institutions, you will likely notice how closely connected they are to American efforts to groom Muslim moderates. There are typically publicity materials at these events that indicate, for example, that these civil society organizations receive program funding from American sources like USAID, the Fulbright program, or the Ford Foundation, or that they work closely with groups like the Asia Foundation, a U.S.-based nonprofit organization focusing on issues of democracy and development. It would be reductive, however, to regard Indonesian civil society activists as mere agents of post-9/11 American projects of empire. Rather, the collaborations with American partners are useful for Indonesians who are themselves concerned about the rise of religious conservatism domestically since the New Order's collapse.

The civil society organizations advocating for religious freedom are staffed by activists from liberal Muslim student groups like Formaci. Rizal, for example, interned in one of these organizations while he was an undergraduate and became a full-time employee when he graduated. Hired as an assistant editor, Rizal had the primary responsibility of overseeing the publication of magazines serving as a rebuttal to the conservative print media that were proliferating among the reading public. Flipping through some of the magazine issues he has published, I discovered articles with titles like "The Ethics of Quranic Recitation: Text and Context," "Democracy Protects Religious Freedom," and "The Origins of Conservatism and Fundamentalism in Islam." It is of course no coincidence that these articles share similar themes with the discussions in Formaci's study circles—in fact, Rizal acknowledged that he has brought the understanding of liberal Islam that he acquired in university to his job in the NGO. In addition to his publishing duties, Rizal occasionally participated in the NGO's *sosialisasi* or "socialization" programs, which were usually seminars that teach important cultural influencers such as university students and madrasa teachers the foundations of progressive Islam. He was, in short, advancing moderate Islam at the front lines.

Based on post-9/11 Western projects of religious tolerance, liberal Muslims are seen as the legitimate spokespersons of religious moderation, while conservative Islamists are regarded as the proponents of intolerance and violence. In other words, clear lines have been drawn to separate those people, beliefs, and practices that count as moderate from the others that do not. The assumption is that religion is a stable and independent sphere where such precise demarcations can be made. The religion that I have described in the preceding chapters, however, is far from stable or self-contained. Since the political transition from authoritarianism to democracy, Muslims from across the ideological spectrum have been experimenting with new ways of practicing Islam as they seek to translate between the ideals attached to their religion and those of Western liberalism. Part-Muslim, part-Western religious practices have emerged as a result. It is a religion that is contingent on the political and economic situation and whose believers adapt their religious practices to the evolving circumstances of their lives. But what happens when the improvisational and situational aspects of religion are overlooked? Is it effective for the moderate Islam project to attribute violence and discrimination to bad believers who are assumed to be stable, self-contained, and hence easily identifiable subjects?

The Making of Moderate Islam

Two important bodies of religious authority in Indonesia recently announced their respective proposals to create moderate Islam. The first is Nahdlatul Ulama (NU), the largest Muslim organization in Indonesia and possibly the world, with approximately fifty million members. In 2015 it held its thirty-third national congress, with the theme "Reinforcing Islam Nusantara for Indonesia and for international civilization." *Islam Nusantara*, or "Islam of the Archipelago," promotes the notion of an Islam that embraces and adapts to the cultural diversity across the many thousands of islands that make up Indonesia.[2] The second organization advocating for religious moderation is Muhammadiyah, which is the nation's second-largest Muslim organization, with about thirty-five million members. Its forty-seventh national congress, also held in 2015, was billed "Enlightenment for a Progressive Indonesia," a theme adapted from Muhammadiyah's long-standing concept of *Islam berkemajuan*, or "progressive Islam."[3] Both organizations promote their respective understanding of religious moderation through the schools, hospitals, charitable foundations, community centers, and political parties affiliated with each of them. In fact, many of the progressive student groups that I have researched and the NGOs that eventually employ my young informants are associated with either of the two organizations.

NU's and Muhammadiyah's ambitions to become the guardians of religious moderation have received endorsement by the government. Importantly, the government not only supports their domestic efforts but also encourages these organizations to export their models of religious thought and practice to the international arena. Moderate Islam is regarded as a key asset in Indonesian foreign policy. In the post-9/11 context, the government has sought to present Indonesia, the world's most populous Muslim nation and third-largest democracy, as not only progressive and tolerant but also the rightful mediator between the West and Islam. Religious leaders from NU and Muhammadiyah have become diplomats who travel the world to participate in interfaith programs organized by the Indonesian foreign ministry. The government has also backed NU's recent establishment of Bayt ar-Rahmah, a nonprofit organization based in Winston-Salem, North Carolina, which will be the base for its international efforts to promote Indonesian-style religious moderation. Additionally, NU will collaborate with Austria's University of Vienna, which tracks and examines ISIS propaganda, to prepare and disseminate responses to those messages.[4]

Despite current collaborations among NU, Muhammadiyah, and the Indonesian government to create moderate Islam, the relationships between these two religious entities have historically been complicated and adversarial. NU and Muhammadiyah have long opposed each other on how to be Muslim in modern society. NU promotes traditionalism, or that Muslims must defer to the authority of religious scholars, while Muhammadiyah advocates for modernism, or the ability of Muslims to engage in scriptural interpretation independently of scholars. It is only recently, however, that these old rivals have joined forces to prevent the Islamists, a relatively new arrival in the religious and political scene, from becoming the standard-bearers of Indonesian Islam. Even though they have accused the Islamists of intolerance, NU and Muhammadiyah are deeply heterogeneous organizations that contain factions that are progressive and conservative and have gone through periods of tolerance and intolerance. In 1965, for example, NU collaborated with the Indonesian military to kill ordinary citizens suspected of being Communists, paving the way for the rise of the New Order. A subsequent period of violent repression by the New Order led NU to withdraw from electoral politics in the 1980s and reinvent itself as a progressive, civil society critic of the government (see Hefner 2000 for details).

While NU and Muhammadiyah are among the organizations that have stepped into the role of spokespersons for moderate Islam, other organizations have been singled out as proponents of bad Islam. Progressive NGOs, like the one where Rizal worked, play an important role in identifying these targets of reform. When I visited him at his office one day, Rizal was in the midst of preparing a report that attributed the recent proliferation of religious conservatism and fundamentalism to the Indonesian Council of Religious Scholars (Majelis Ulama Indonesia, or MUI). The MUI is a quasi-governmental body that functions as the primary fatwa-issuing body in Indonesia. When it was founded in 1975 by the New Order, the MUI issued fatwas that supported the interests of the secular national regime. However, as Rizal's report argues, there has been a distinct conservative turn in the organization since the democratic transition. For example, the MUI compiled a list of fourteen groups that it believes have deviated from the Islamic creed, including the Ahmadiyah and the Shi'a. The MUI has also issued a fatwa against secularism, pluralism, and liberalism—which it labels with the acronym "SIPILIS" so as to liken these principles to the venereal disease—to censure the activities of progressive NGOs like the Liberal Islam Network.[5]

Progressive NGOs compile qualitative and quantitative data on the misbehavior of bad Muslim actors. Rizal, for example, kept a binder of newspaper reports to document the spread of religious conservatism. In his binder were stories about vigilante groups raiding food stalls that remain open in the daytime during Ramadan, national television stations pixelating videos and photos of female celebrities who show too much skin, conservative politicians using condemnatory rhetoric on gays and lesbians, and religious leaders forbidding Muslims from observing non-Muslim holidays, even if it is to wish "Merry Christmas" or "Happy Chinese New Year" to those celebrating. Such news reports allow NGOs to compile statistics on religious violence and discrimination, categories that have only begun to be tracked in the democratic era. For instance, Setara Institute, a Jakarta-based organization that conducts research on democracy, noted 220 cases of violent attacks on religious minorities in 2013, which was an increase from 91 similar incidents in 2007.[6] These statistics get cited by international human rights organizations like Human Rights Watch and serve as an assessment of Indonesia's moderate Muslim status. Given how these statistics portray an uptick in religion-based conflicts in recent years, international commentators have begun to cast doubt on Indonesia's reputation as moderate, writing op-eds with titles such as "Is Indonesia Really the World's Most Tolerant Muslim Country?"[7] and "No Model for Muslim Democracy."[8]

Concerns that Indonesia's moderation is in jeopardy have given rise to the popular discourse on Indonistan. As Indonesians watched conservative Islamists seeking to introduce symbols of Muslim authenticity attributed to the early Muslim communities in Mecca and Medina, from big beards and loose tunics to a strict compliance with sharia law, many wondered if their nation was losing its cultural identity and becoming more like Afghanistan and Pakistan. Many Indonesians were especially concerned about the activities of the right-wing vigilante group Islamic Defenders Front (Front Pembela Islam, or FPI). Founded shortly after the collapse of the New Order, the FPI sought to enact sharia law by raiding places of immorality like bars, brothels, and gambling dens, assaulting progressive activists rallying in support of religious freedom, murdering members of the Ahmadiyah, and evicting Christians from their churches. The FPI was established by Habib Rizieq Shihab, an Indonesian religious preacher of Arab descent who claims a lineage to the Prophet Muhammad. Apart from this supposed ancestral relationship, the organization does not appear to have ties to the Arab world. The organization is backed by local funders, including top army generals who wish to cultivate it as a militant counter to civil society organizations investigating military crimes and other abuses of power (Jahroni 2004).

Popular narratives often emphasize the FPI's foreignness, even though the organization is deeply embedded in post–New Order machinations of power. A prominent example is the satirical Facebook page titled "Anda Bertanya Habib Rizieq Menjawab" (You Ask, Habib Rizieq Answers), which swiftly acquired more than one hundred thousand followers when it was set up in 2011.[9] Through the use of cartoons, digitally altered images, and news reports, the page frequently targets Habib Rizieq's Arab ancestry. He is portrayed as someone who rides a camel in urban Jakarta. He peppers his speech with Arabic words—for example, to say "I," he will use the Arabic *ana* instead of the Indonesian *saya* or *aku*. To accentuate his Arabness, he pronounces the letter *p* as *f*—for example, he refers to the "parody page" as a "farody fage," and his favorite phrase, "Ana pentung!" (I'll whack you!) is changed to "Ana fentung!" This is done in order to produce the f-f-f affectation, which is the Indonesian stereotype of what Arab speech sounds like. The FPI disciples of Habib Rizieq are portrayed as idiots. They are described as "two digiters," which refers to people with a sub-one-hundred IQ—in contrast, ordinary Indonesians are referred to as "three digiters," or people who possess a normal level of intelligence. The ideological work accomplished by these descriptions is to define Indonistan as a zone of religious intolerance and utter stupidity, and to locate it outside Indonesia—more specifically, as a "-stan," it is to be found in the presumably backward and turbulent region of Central Asia and the Middle East.

The discourse of Indonistan reveals the political cost of making the argument about moderate Indonesia. The *New York Times* puts it best when it declares that "Indonesia offers the Muslim world a model quite different from that of Middle Eastern regimes."[10] In other words, if Indonesia represents good Islam, then culpability for bad Islam is assigned to the Middle East and Central Asia. It is certainly true that conservative and exclusivist ideologies like Salafism and Wahhabism and radical groups like al-Qaeda and ISIS emerged from the Arab world and that Saudi Arabia is quite possibly the largest state sponsor of Islamist terrorists. These developments have created negative ripple effects in Indonesia—for example, as young men volunteer themselves for jihadist causes. Yet religious conservatism and extremism cannot simply be attributed to an Arab culture that is often stereotyped as brusque, tribal, and misogynist. Rather, they need to be seen in relation to political and economic factors, such as the repeated American military interventions in the Middle East and Central Asia from the Cold War to the more recent War on Terror (Mamdani 2004), which have been driven by the disastrous mix of failed intelligence and the quest for oil and power. In other words, Western projects of empire are deeply implicated in the emergence of conservative and extremist forms of Islam.

Are Islamists Bad Muslims? (Part 1)

Instead of recognizing how religion intersects with other spheres like politics and economics, the moderate Muslim paradigm attributes the problems in Muslim societies to bad believers, particularly conservative Islamists. Gender-based oppressions like honor killings and disfigurement, for example, are widely regarded as an outcome of Islamist opposition to the ideals of Western feminism (Abu-Lughod 2013). Such explanations are prevalent in Indonesia, as I discovered when I attended a seminar organized by the Prosperous Justice Party titled "Preparing Women to Become the Nation's Pillars." In his keynote address, the party's then secretary-general Anis Matta urged more women to take up leadership positions rather than remaining passive followers. This was hardly the first time party leaders complained about a lack of female leadership. Former party chairman Hidayat Nur Wahid has also conveyed his disappointment that only 10 percent of the party's representatives voted into the House of Representatives were women, even though women constituted 57 percent of the party's supporters (Muhtadi 2006). Several progressive activists who were present at the seminar speculated that the dearth of women leaders in the Islamist movement was a reflection of its overarching anti-women attitude. One of them even urged me to write an essay titled "Gender and Violence among the Islamists." (In fact, for the entire duration of my fieldwork, this person would consistently suggest that I add the suffix "and violence" when writing about any topic pertaining to Islamists.)

However, as I investigated gender relations among the conservative Islamists, I discovered that it is far too simplistic to cast them in the role of bad Muslims who oppose gender equality. While student activism has traditionally been a male domain, the Campus Proselytization Association provides opportunity for young women to participate in important public conversations on religion and politics. It is one of the few student organizations that attracts fairly equal numbers of male and female participants. From this perspective, the disappointment expressed by top Islamist politicians regarding the absence of female leaders is understandable. How are we to understand women's attraction to Islamist activism? One contributing factor is that Indonesian women have long played important public roles in the reproduction of Islam. Anna Gade (2004), for example, argues that women are regarded as maestros of Quranic recitation and memorization in Indonesian society. Similarly, Pieternella van Doorn-Harder (2006) points out that while madrasas are traditionally reserved for men, Indonesian women have been able to study in madrasas and eventually become professors in Islamic universities. Women also participate in mass Muslim organizations like NU and Muhammadiyah, where they have had some success in persuading male religious leaders to take women's issues seriously.

The broadening of women's roles and identities in the democratic era is another important factor influencing women's participation in the Islamist movement. During the New Order, women were discouraged from being politically active (or even too publicly religious, as seen in how women were banned from wearing head scarfs in schools and other governmental institutions). Gender roles were defined according to the New Order's conception of the heteronormative family that formed the foundation of the nation—male head of household, a largely domestic woman who prioritizes her duties as wife and mother, and two children (Boellstorff 2005, 195). To the citizens, Indonesia was presented as a scaled-up version of this ideal family where Suharto was the father figure (*bapak*) who must be obeyed. The popular media played an important role in normalizing the gender roles defined by the New Order. Film studies scholar Intan Paramaditha (2007) observes that there is a tendency in Indonesian films made during this political context to portray women as one-dimensional characters—"idealized versions of femininity or 'fallen women' in need of moral reform and redemption"—or, in typical New Order fashion, "as supporters of men and the state who, despite their activities in the public sphere, did not forget their 'nature' as mothers and wives."

Women's roles and identities were redefined following the fall of the New Order, with the establishment of numerous civil society organizations that worked within the ambit of secular feminism and championed issues like human rights, gender equality, and women's reproductive rights, and the rise in political activism by conservative Islamist women.[11] Parallel changes were also seen in the popular media, with the emergence of films with feminist themes in which the central characters were women who were portrayed with depth and nuance. Intan Paramaditha examines one such film, *Pasir Berbisik*, where the mother is protective but does not conform to idealized models of femininity and thus challenges the stereotype of the *ibu* (mother) who was portrayed by the New Order as nurturing and self-sacrificing. In fact, Paramaditha, who is also a writer of fantasy fiction (2015), directly contributes to the shifting landscape of gender by penning short stories about complex female characters—a hideous ghost who transformed herself into a beautiful girl to seduce a handsome hunter, a doting mother with one lover after another, middle-aged aunties who lust after a male youth with curly hair and strong cheekbones—each of whom "hid love, longing, sickness, desire, anger; spinning, her determined passions without stopping, without end."

Likewise, when I asked why they participated in the Campus Proselytization Association, young Islamist women expressed a desire to explore the various roles and identities that had become available to them in the democratic era. My research assistant Nuriya was attracted to the organization because of its emphasis on the development of strong and capable women. Along with other female recruits, Nuriya had to undergo a grueling orientation camp aimed at character building, where she was awakened late one night to go for a "night walk." A popular activity among young campers in Indonesia, the night walk requires that camp participants traverse a dark forested area and perform certain tasks, while steeling themselves in the presence of the forest's denizens, whether fauna or phantom, for purposes of developing courage. Nuriya and her friends were eventually led to a river in the forest and ordered to wade through it. "To be brave Muslim women who can carry out God's commands, you need to be able to conquer all challenges in life!" shouted a camp counselor who was a more senior undergraduate. Nuriya refused, arguing that the activity was nothing more than hazing. She had read many Islamic liturgical texts and was confident that none of those texts mentioned a cold river as being instrumental in the formation of piety. Outraged at being challenged, the camp counselor shoved Nuriya into the river and forced her to remain submerged for a few minutes.

Although she hated the camp experience, Nuriya gradually came to appreciate that the organization's female participants carry the same burden of expectations as their male counterparts. Both female and male cadres were supposed to carry out their religious obligations diligently, take part in street protests and other public conversations on politics, get good grades (a minimum GPA score of 3.0), win scholarships and other academic prizes, attend job-hunting workshops, and eventually land good jobs. Both sexes were also required to demonstrate the bureaucratic capabilities and leadership skills necessary for religious outreach. In 2009, a few days before Ramadan began, female participants at the University of Indonesia organized a "Wear the Hijab" campaign. Free head scarfs were distributed to encourage other female undergraduates to keep their hair covered for the entire duration of the holy month. Preparation for the campaign began months earlier. Led by the committee on women's affairs in the student organization, the female activists raised funds (by seeking donations from alumni members of the organization and selling homemade women's fashion accessories like brooches), designed publicity posters, and searched for wholesale retailers from whom they could purchase head scarfs at reasonable prices.[12] In other words, values like individual discipline, entrepreneurship, and self-actualization are embraced by conservative Islamist women.

Importantly, however, Islamist discourses of femininity also diverge from liberal feminism.[13] Nuriya explained to me that the Islamist movement emphasized the continuous self-improvement of both women and men, because the creation of strong and capable Muslim individuals (*ishlah an-nafs*) is the first step toward the creation of pious families (*ishlah al-bait al-muslim*), a pious society (*ishlah al-mujtama'*, and eventually, a pious nation-state (*ishlah al-hukumah*). In this formulation, it is the community that should be the ultimate beneficiary of skilled individuals, not the individual herself (see also Deeb 2006). Furthermore, although the Islamist movement wants both its female and male activists to be exceptional, it believes in a God-given hierarchy of the sexes and hence does not groom men and women to be equals. Young female activists were expected to possess leadership and bureaucratic skills, but they were only allowed to lead other women. The highest position that a woman can occupy in the Campus Proselytization Association is the chair of the committee on women's affairs, whereas all other important leadership positions must be occupied only by men. Thus, while the moderate Muslim paradigm categorizes Muslims into those who are either for or against liberal values, the practices of the conservative Islamists suggest that Muslim realities are far messier, given that they can simultaneously accept and reject liberal values.

Are Islamists Bad Muslims? (Part 2)

To better understand if gender-based oppression ought to be blamed on the Islamists, let us examine further the interactions between men and women in the Campus Proselytization Association. Islamists place great emphasis on modesty, as I discovered during interviews with female activists, who would always insist that my research assistant Nuriya be present as chaperone. In one interview after another, the interviewees would answer my questions but fix their gaze on Nuriya while completely avoiding eye contact with me. These projects to create cadres who are guarded in the presence of the opposite sex are informed by Quranic verses on modesty.[14] Islamists are critical of Indonesian laxity with regard to interactions between men and women, citing, for example, how Indonesian men and women seem to be more willing to shake hands with one another, compared to Muslims elsewhere. Islamists are also quick to criticize the top politicians in their own party when they fail to behave properly with the opposite sex. One example is the information minister Tifatul Sembiring, a major proponent of the modesty movement who claims to have restricted his interactions with women out of piety and blames natural disasters in Indonesia on lack of modesty among Indonesians. In 2010, Sembiring was lambasted by other Islamists for shaking hands with U.S. First Lady Michelle Obama during her visit to Indonesia. Defending himself from accusations of hypocrisy, Sembiring alleged that Mrs. Obama forced the physical contact.

Participants in the Campus Proselytization Association used various techniques to separate men and women. In events held in large lecture halls, men were seated either in front or on the right, which is regarded as the cleaner side, while women were positioned at the back or on the left. In more intimate settings like administrative meetings involving a few people, a makeshift barrier would be constructed between men and women. During one such meeting that I attended, a banner for a past event was tied between two pillars, separating the men and women who sat on the floor on either side of the banner. A whiteboard was placed on the floor, with half the board in the men's sitting area and the other half in the women's. That way the board could be slid into the women's area if they wanted to see the notes that the men wrote on it, and vice versa. I asked whether it was odd to have a discussion when one cannot see half the participants involved, but everyone seemed to affirm the benefits of the barrier. Women said that the barrier enabled meetings to proceed more quickly and smoothly, since it prevented the men from teasing or flirting with them. Men, on the other hand, said that the barrier allowed women to overcome their shyness about speaking up, since it shielded them from the men's gaze; this supposedly resulted in a more productive discussion.

Such physical barriers may be effective for regulating interactions in confined spaces like rooms, but not for interactions that occurred outdoors, or on the Internet or over the phone. In those situations, the Islamist students would have to create other types of barriers (note that the Arabic term for barrier is *hijab*). For example, they were taught by their mentors and religious teachers to send text messages or chat online with one another for urgent organizational purposes only, and only during daylight hours. Another method is called the barrier of the eyes (*hijab mata*), which is when men and women avoid eye contact when talking to one another. Instead of discreetly lowering their gazes during conversations, which is rather conventional in Muslim societies, Islamists perform more exaggerated versions where one person is looking toward the ceiling while the other at the floor, or where both have their backs toward the other. The point of these disciplinary practices is for the cadres to develop a barrier around the heart (*hijab hati*), which is the ability to controls one's heart so as not to develop romantic or sexual feelings for the person with whom one frequently has close contact.

Religious teachers in the Islamist movement informed me that the primary target of the various techniques of separation is men's sexual desires (*hawa nafsu*). They cited many authoritative jurisprudential opinions that portrayed men as libidinous creatures (women, on the other hand, were regarded as objects of desire but were thought to possess no sexual desire of their own). For instance, some classical scholars have said that a wife must immediately comply with her husband's demands for sex, even when she is doing work in the kitchen or when they are both still riding a camel, while other scholars opine that angels will curse the woman who spurns her husband's advances.[15] The underlying assumption in these jurisprudential opinions is that the husband has the right to his wife's sexual services since he provides sustenance for her. Unlike married men, however, bachelors did not have a permissible outlet for their sexual urges. For bachelors to control their libido and prevent fornication (*zina*), classical religious scholars recommend that they perform supererogatory fasts on Mondays and Thursdays.

Preventing fornication is the ultimate goal of Islamist practices governing interactions between the sexes. Illicit sexual relationships were regarded to be so heinous that some Islamist religious teachers have ranked such relationships as the second gravest sin a person can commit—the gravest being murder. As a precaution against fornication, young Islamists were prohibited from dating (*pacaran*). Not only should they refrain from boyfriend-girlfriend relationships—young men and women were also expected to avoid dating-like behavior, such as sending flirtatious text messages or spending time together for non-organizational purposes (for example, studying in pairs or having lunch together). To reinforce the anti-dating message, religious teachers also encouraged students to read books that discussed the ills of dating, including a publication that was given to me titled "Dating? Yuck, No Thanks!" (Pacaran? Iiiih, Nggak Banget!). In such literature, dating is typically described as an immature form of relationship that two people enter into for casual fun and is therefore devoid of concrete ties and responsibilities to one another. Dating is said to cause negative behavior in people, including fornication, lying to parents, and neglecting daily tasks. Dating is regarded to be so dangerous to one's spiritual health that my young informants referred to it as "the pink virus" (virus merah jambu), pink being the color they associate with the heart.

Similar to Christian abstinence campaigns, Islamist prohibitions on dating do not entirely succeed in preventing youths from forming romantic relationships. If they were caught dating, however, the young Islamists would be punished. Religious teachers in the organization may temporarily suspend their membership and revoke certain privileges, or ask them to memorize a certain number of Quranic verses and hadiths. Nuriya told me a story about how a religious teacher discovered that she, Nuriya, had become close to a male peer. It was regarded as a particularly serious transgression, because her paramour was a committee member in the student organization and former chairman of a prominent Islamist organization in high school and hence expected to be exemplary in behavior. The young man faced a panel consisting of religious teachers and student leaders, where he was questioned about photographs in which he and Nuriya were captured together in the same frame. None of these photographs, which were taken at organizational events and had numerous people posing for the camera, would typically be considered inappropriate. But the panel regarded them as adequate evidence to substantiate rumors about the couple. To save himself, the young man told the panel that Nuriya was the one who pursued him. It may have helped to blame her. He was allowed to retain his position in the organization, but she was barred from taking on any position of significance. Furious with the betrayal, Nuriya lost romantic interest in him.

To curb potential problems regarding immodesty, Islamist religious teachers often encouraged young Islamists to get married quickly. Marriages should ideally be arranged through a matchmaking process called the *taaruf* (which is Arabic for "introduction").[16] Zainab, a twenty-two-year-old classmate of Nuriya, had just finished writing her senior thesis when the matchmaking process was initiated for her. She had never gone on a date because she thought it was not virtuous, but now that she was about to join the working world, she decided that she was ready for marriage. With her parents' blessings, Zainab asked her religious teacher to find her a partner. The religious teacher then approached other religious teachers for potential names. For the sake of attaining the highest level of respectability, religious teachers will try to match two Islamist cadres who are likely to have never met before—for example, who lived in different cities, studied in different universities, or were from different cohorts or different faculties within the same university. Matches set between two people from the same social circle could be problematic because they sometimes invited rumors that the couple had been dating and were now trying to make amends by getting married.

A potential match for Zainab was found in Bogor, a college town just south of Jakarta that is an important hub for Islamist student activism. The Islamist matchmaking process made use of the bureaucratic practices associated with a job search, as the religious teacher asked Zainab to prepare a curriculum vitae detailing her educational background, organizational responsibilities, and work experience, as well as personal information such as family background and hobbies. A photograph of Zainab taken against a white background, standard for a passport application, was also attached. While matchmaking is obviously not a new practice in Indonesia, the use of the curriculum vitae is a recent innovation that reflects the influence Western bureaucratic practices have had on the Islamist movement in democratic and neoliberal Indonesia. In terms of the sequence of exchange, the woman's curriculum vitae is sent to the man first. The man has the first right of refusal, as his information will be sent to her only if he likes what he sees. Zainab received her potential suitor's curriculum vitae after two weeks, not a long time, but just long enough for her to be tormented by the possibility of rejection by someone who would always remain a mystery to her.

If the woman reciprocates the man's interest in her, the prospective couple will meet for the first time at the woman's house, together with her parents and the matchmaking religious teachers, mimicking the interview stage of a job search. The couple can grill one another on any range on topics, including their habits and personalities, knowledge of the religious scriptures, and opinions on current affairs. I was skeptical of whether young Islamists could make a decision on matrimonial compatibility based on a conversation closely scrutinized by adults, but religious teachers assured me that people who are ready for marriage will answer the questions sincerely and honestly. They claimed that the conversation is more transparent than the communication between boyfriends and girlfriends, since dating is supposedly based on lust and ultimately full of deceit. After the meeting, the prospective couple must perform the *solat istihorah* prayers to ask for a divine signal regarding whether they should proceed with marriage. Although it is common for people to decline the match after the interview, there were rumors of couples who felt pressure to get married and not embarrass their parents and the religious teachers who arranged the match. When a couple agrees to marry, their families must arrange the wedding quickly. As their wedding date approaches, the prospective bride and groom are allowed to communicate with each other by telephone and spend time together in the presence of family members.

Zainab's potential suitor was disappointed when she rejected him after the interview. "Was he ugly?" I asked. "No, actually he's quite cute," she chuckled. "But I got really scared about marrying someone I barely know." Such fears regarding the matchmaking process explain why some young Islamists preferred to find their own partners through illicit dating. Others relied on a method called "tagging" (*nge-tag*), which is regarded as a compromise between dating and matchmaking. This means that a man would approach a female friend whom he fancies, profess his feelings for her, and ask if she would consider him as a potential husband. If she agrees, he would seek permission to marry her from her parents. Compared to matchmaking, "tagging" gives the young man more control over the identity of his bride, but like matchmaking, the young woman can never make the first move. Regardless of how partnerships are formed, Islamists generally believed that marriages should not be delayed. A male student activist, who did not have a prospective partner during the time of my fieldwork but was looking for one to "tag," told me that he did not want to graduate with what he termed "double bachelors"—a bachelor's degree and the status of an unmarried man.

There appears to be significant consequences of rushing young people into marriage. I knew three married couples, all of whom were still in college or had recently graduated, who told me that they were experiencing severe financial difficulties. Complaints about money were common among recent graduates in Jakarta, where starting monthly salaries are often less than US$300, about a quarter of which is spent on rent alone. But perhaps the strain is felt more acutely by Islamist couples, who often got married before either spouse had attained some kind of economic security and who had children soon after marriage, since populating the world with new Muslims is regarded as an important form of religious proselytization. Many Islamists frown on contraceptives, and some couples have several children within a span of several years, even though there are a plurality of views about birth control among Indonesian religious scholars, and since the 1980s some organizations have issued fatwas permitting the use of birth control (Doorn-Harder 2006, 13). In instances where the couple do not receive help from their parents, it is the wife that gives up the pursuit of a career as she either works part time or becomes a full-time homemaker to care for the children, while the family subsists largely on the income of the husband.

The decision-making processes in these young families could help us understand the frustrations expressed by top Islamist leaders regarding why so few Islamist women become social and political leaders. To recapitulate, the Prosperous Justice Party poured a lot of resources into the Campus Proselytization Association to groom new generations of Islamist activists. The training programs run by the student organization aimed to maximize the potential of both male and female undergraduates. The training programs did not promote equality among the sexes, but this did not mean that they rejected liberal feminism entirely. Rather, the programs seemed to operate on a hybrid model that Pieternella van Doorn-Harder terms "Islamist feminism," which is concerned with women's empowerment but stresses male authority over women, complementarity rather than equality between men and women, and sharia law as the determinant of women's rights (2006, 7–8). Given the emphasis that Islamists place on maintaining strict moral codes in male-female relations, the young activists are urged to marry early, which leads the young women who have been trained to become future social and political leaders to become housewives instead. In other words, the lack of female leadership in the Islamist movement cannot simply be attributed to the misogyny of bad believers. Rather, these slippages could be seen as an effect of religious improvisation, or those adaptations that religious believers make when they encounter different ethical systems whose outcomes cannot be determined in advance.

Beyond "Religious" Violence

Conservative Islamists are certainly capable of violence, including those acts of coercion and discrimination targeted at women. When political power was decentralized from Jakarta following the transition to democracy, Islamist politicians helped to introduce sharia-inspired regional bylaws targeting immorality. Women were the primary object of discipline. For example, bylaws in Pamekasan (East Java Province), Gowa (South Sulawesi Province), Cianjur (West Java Province), and Padang (West Sumatra Province) state that women must wear the head scarf in schools and offices. In Gorontalo (North Sulawesi Province), women are prohibited from being in public alone after midnight. In Tangerang (West Java Province), women could be arrested for prostitution if found in public places after women's curfew hours have begun. Of the regions that have implemented sharia law, Aceh Province is perhaps the best known. Women in Aceh could be fined by the morality police if caught without a head scarf in public and are banned from straddling a motorbike behind a male driver (they are told to close their legs and ride sidesaddle instead). Along with their male partners, women have also been publicly flogged for suspicion of fornication (Budiman 2008). Islamists' support for the bylaws seems to be at variance with their support of women's self-actualization programs, but this is unsurprising, given that human beings are well able to live unperturbed with contradictions in their lives.

Instead of being a self-contained sphere, religion expresses itself in relation to other domains of social life, including work, play, and governance. Whether they promote the empowerment or subjugation of women, Islamist actions are always informed by the political context they inhabit. Importantly, Islamist support of sharia bylaws targeting immorality must be understood in relation to how secular politicians have also backed these very laws in order to boost their own popularity. There is a precedent of secular politicians in the nation pandering to religious conservatism for political leverage (though obviously this is neither unique to

Islam nor Indonesia). The most famous example, as stated earlier, is how Suharto tried to gain the support of Muslim conservatives in the 1990s by performing Muslimness—for example, by going on pilgrimage to Mecca, opening Islamic banks, and removing Christian ministers from his cabinet. In the post-Suharto era, Islamist support of sharia bylaws disciplining women must be understood in relation to how the democratic Indonesian government permits misogyny in its agencies. For instance, the police and military still require female job applicants to undergo a "two-finger" test to check whether their hymen is intact. The procedure assumes that a woman's virginity makes her more emotionally stable and hence more able to perform the job competently.[17] As this example suggests, conservative Islamists do not have a monopoly over sexism.

Historically, there have been deep entanglements between religion, gender, and nationalism in Indonesian politics. During the anticommunist purge that brought him to the presidency, Suharto ordered the extermination of the most significant women's organization of the time, Gerwani (an acronym for Gerakan Wanita Indonesia, or the Indonesian Women's Movement). Founded in 1950, Gerwani was well known for its brand of socialist feminism whose activists rejected polygamy, defended the rights of female laborers, and petitioned for legal reforms to ensure greater protection for female citizens. By 1965, it attracted 1.5 million members across the nation. The same year, however, the military disseminated propaganda that Gerwani's activists were participating in sex parties, dancing naked in public, working as prostitutes, and castrating military generals—claims that today's historians argue are unfounded. These reports stoked the fury of anticommunist groups, which began popularizing slogans like "Gerwani tjabol" (Gerwani whores), "Gantung Gerwani" (Hang Gerwani), and "Ganjang Gerwani" (Crush Gerwani), before raping and killing the women activists. The New Order often cited Gerwani as a shameful example of feminine immorality and decadence. As an alternative, the regime conceptualized the *ibu* (mother) as the ideal woman, domestic and politically defanged (Wieringa 2003).

One of the most significant lessons of the anticommunist purge is that violence is a child of many parents. The killings may have been orchestrated by the military but were supported by university students who believed that communism threatened secular nationalism, and by religious teachers and madrasa students who believed that communism threatened

Islam. According to Intan Paramaditha, "The military campaigns were so pervasive that many of the fathers and grandfathers of young Indonesians today who did not directly participate in the killings nonetheless supported them, some actively, others passively. In any event, the vast majority of those who lived through 1965–1966 took part in the creation of the New Order regime and thus share the burden of its crime through involuntary silence. The Communist massacre, in other words, is a collective guilt" (2014, 47). National reckoning for this history of violence has only just begun. And the occurrences of violent conflict and discrimination in the present day can be understood as a product of Indonesia's deeply fractured history as the nation struggles to remake its identity in the post–New Order period. Yet analyses of violence in contemporary Indonesia, which are dominated by the discourses of moderate Indonesia and Indonistan and concepts like "religious violence" and "religious intolerance," problematically attribute violence to religion and problematically assume that violence is located outside of the secular.[18]

I have discovered that violence committed in the name of religion is often tangled up in complicated ways with Western liberal ideas about individual liberty and entrepreneurship. I managed to spend some time with several young males in the Islamic Defenders Front (FPI), the vigilante group responsible for much damage and bloodshed in the efforts to uphold sharia law. Gaining access was surprisingly easy, as it took only one phone call for me to get permission to visit them. The group is based in Petamburan, a Jakarta neighborhood popular with Indonesians of Arab descent, which is where the group's founder Habib Rizieq Shihab grew up and maintained a residence. I was invited to a small house that served as the headquarters of one of FPI's youth wings. My hosts were four young men who were about twenty years old, all of whom stopped schooling at around the ninth or tenth grade and expressed no desire to continue with their education. They wore FPI's all-white uniform, though one of them took off his shirt to reveal a pink undershirt (which said "Esprit," a popular brand in Asia) and a large, elaborate tattoo on his right arm. While these youths were friendly, I could not help but feel a sense of revulsion, partly because there was a poster of Osama bin Laden on the wall, but also because a rat ran over my bare foot while I was in the filthy living room. These youths certainly did not fit the stereotype of Muslims who are obsessed with cleanliness and ablution.

When it was nearly time for the *Maghrib* early evening prayers, my hosts took me to a neighborhood mosque that served as the FPI's spiritual center. The prayers were usually followed by a weekly sermon delivered by Habib Rizieq Shihab, but since he was away during my visit, one of his deputies appeared in his place. "Are you coming in?" I asked the young men just as the congregational prayers were about to begin. "Later," one of them said. I sat right beside the entrance to the prayer hall and did not notice any of them walk in to participate in the congregational prayers. Once the prayers were over, I immediately went outside and saw that they had set up a table with many kinds of radical Islamist paraphernalia. The young men were selling posters and badges of Osama bin Laden, T-shirts with a logo of the FPI, DVDs of sermons by right-wing imams, and even a video game set in post-9/11 Iraq where one could play the role of a jihadi combating the invading American military. I asked them whether they were raising funds for the FPI. "No, we're not," someone replied. "This is our own business."

The bulk of the FPI's membership consists of gangsters known in Indonesia as *preman*. The *preman* works odd jobs, for example as a parking attendant or traffic marshal in areas controlled by his gang, or as a busker on public buses who sometimes coerces passengers for tips. Throughout modern Indonesian history, the *preman* has also been utilized by the state, political groups, and religious groups to carry out their dirty work, such as threatening and killing their opponents. The *preman* traces a genealogy to the *vrijman* (Dutch for "free man"), a particular type of economic subject in the Dutch East Indies. Loren Ryter (1998) argues that the *vrijman* was someone who was not in the service of the Dutch East India Company (VOC) but had permission to be in the colonial Indies and carry out trade for the sake of the VOC. He was a free agent, as he was a trader who was not listed on the company payroll. Similarly, when the *preman* participates in the FPI, he is not simply prohibiting the religious freedom of others, but is also exercising the entrepreneurial freedom to sell his muscles. The *preman* thus shares the experiences of other lower-working-class young men around the world who, as Jean and John Comaroff have argued (2000), are increasingly shut out by the neoliberal economy (which prefers cheaper feminized labor) and must hustle in the informal economy instead. Their brand of radical Islam is also situational and improvisational.

In 2012, when I returned to Jakarta for a visit, I managed to interview one of the co-creators of the satirical Facebook page "You Ask, Habib

Rizieq Answers," which has become one of the FPI's most vocal critics in popular culture. We met at a trendy coffee shop after he ran a background check to ensure that I was not an FPI Trojan horse. A recent university graduate working at a technology start-up firm, he created the page with three other friends in the same company. He had been involved with several local civil society organizations that had ties to the American project of religious freedom, and was inspired to use humor as a weapon to undermine the FPI's legitimacy in light of the government's inability to shut down the group. I was sympathetic with his activist efforts to undermine vigilante violence, but it also occurred to me that during the time of our interview, Indonesians had been choking for months from smoke caused by the burning of the nation's rain forests. Suharto opened the nation to local and transnational entrepreneurs who conducted mining and logging and established plantations for cash crops with high global demand like oil palm, and whose activities have accelerated further under the neoliberal economic reforms that accompanied Indonesia's transition to democracy (Li 2007; Tsing 2005). I began to wonder if the discourses of moderate Indonesia and Indonistan, by shining a spotlight on violence linked to Islam, mask the other types of harm plaguing Indonesians, like the violence of economic liberalism.

EPILOGUE

The student activists of this book, like Rizal, Hassan, and Nuriya, were part of the first generation of Indonesians to come of age following Indonesia's transition from authoritarianism to democracy. Energized by the new political and economic freedoms of the era, youths of various ideological orientations gathered in autodidactic reading circles to debate religion independently of established religious and political authorities and invent new ways of being Muslim through play and trial and error. Hybrid forms of religious practices emerged as a result, some of which seem strange and contrary to all expectations. The youths adopted accounting and auditing technologies borrowed from the business world to enforce discipline in the performance of Islamic religious rituals. They switched back and forth between reading the Quran and the works of great Western thinkers, from Aristotle to Hegel and Marx, in order to reinterpret the holy sources through the lens of Western social scientific and humanities literature. They tried to reconcile secular feminist ideals with Islamic demands on modesty. They also joined piety movements, political parties, and nongovernmental organizations to influence the terms of public debate on religion and politics. These youths, in short, were at the forefront of imagining what it means to be Muslim in a world where liberal values had been enlarged.

Student activism appears to have left an indelible mark on the lives of my primary informants, particularly in their career choices. Since the conclusion of my research, all my informants have received their undergraduate degrees, and some have even embarked on their journey toward graduate education; most have gotten married, and some already have several children. Many of them were working in institutions that have close ties with student organizations, and performing jobs that examine and shape the interface between the religious and the secular. Rizal was employed at a liberal Muslim civil society organization concerned with disseminating a pluralist interpretation of Islam. Hassan worked at a social service agency associated with the Prosperous Justice Party that focuses on the collection and disbursement of tithes (*zakat*), and assisted several Islamist politicians in their grassroots outreach projects. Nuriya taught full-time at a madrasa and occasionally contributed to the research activities of a nongovernmental organization concerned with issues pertaining to women and children. All three of them sometimes returned to their respective student organizations to mentor their juniors, and in so doing contribute to the continuation of student political activity in the nation.

I have characterized the Indonesian attempts to reconcile religious and liberal values as "improvisational Islam." The term may seem redundant, given that all religious life is in some senses improvisational and involves groping around to adapt religion to a world that is constantly changing—how else could religion have such a successful career in human history? In the case of Islam in the contemporary world, however, calling attention to the religious improvisation of its adherents is not redundant; it is political. Far too often and for far too long, Muslims have been portrayed as rigid and intractable. My aim has been to show the imaginative labor put in by Muslims to create a habitable life in a world saturated by the power of the West and the ideals of secular liberalism. The religious practices that result from religious improvisation may be surprising because they do not fit into our conception of what Islam looks like. Allowing ourselves to be surprised by Islam is important because it helps us question the assumptions we have about it, assumptions that have not helped to make our world a better place. There is a parallel between the attention I am drawing to "improvisational Islam" and how U.S. activists concerned with police brutality targeting black people call their movement "Black Lives Matter." Of course all lives matter, but in a world where people of color are exterminated systematically, it becomes politically imperative to state that black lives matter.

The particular historical circumstances framing the lives of Indonesian youths help to shine a spotlight on the religious improvisation among them. There is a long precedent of youth participation in religion and politics in Indonesia, in addition to a rich local tradition of dealing with cultural diversity in the archipelago. Furthermore, these youths inhabited a newly democratic context where they have to grapple with the expanded influence of both Islamic and liberal values as well as contend with the decades of authoritarian state violence that has seared itself into the fabric of the nation. In a sense, Indonesia's time of possibility could be regarded as a magnifying glass that brings into sharper relief the processes of religious improvisation that are occurring across Muslim societies. Muslims in today's world cannot escape the hegemony of the West, whether they have migrated to secular democratic countries in Europe and North America, or live in post-colonies where the impact of Western imperialism lingers, or have been touched by the sweeping neoliberal economic reforms of recent decades. While Muslims do not necessarily lead their lives according to the dictates of secular liberalism, the interpretations of their religious scriptures do not occur independently of the values that are cherished by the West. Improvisational Islam is thus everywhere, though perhaps it needs to be noticed more often.

My reluctance to cast improvisational Islam as uniquely Indonesian relates to my skepticism of Indonesia's international reputation as an exemplary moderate Muslim nation. Indonesia gained the reputation after the democratic reforms following Suharto's ouster. For many observers, democratic Indonesia proves that Islam can coexist with secular liberalism and thus offers a beacon of hope in a geopolitical context where Islam had become synonymous with the 9/11 terrorist attacks. Barack Obama, whose mother was an anthropologist who conducted long-term fieldwork in Indonesia, frequently waxes lyrical about his experience growing up there. "I saw it firsthand as a child in Indonesia, where devout Christians worshipped freely in an overwhelmingly Muslim country," he said in Egypt in 2009 in the first speech he made in the Muslim world as U.S. president.[1] When Hillary Clinton visited Indonesia later that year in her capacity as secretary of state, she also spoke about the nation's exemplarity: "If you want to know if Islam, democracy, modernity and women's rights can coexist, go to Indonesia."[2] Likewise, during his visit to Indonesia in 2012, amid the political turmoil of the Arab Spring, British prime minister David Cameron declared, "What Indonesia shows is that in the world's largest Muslim-majority country, it is possible to reject this extremist threat and prove that democracy and Islam can flourish alongside one another."[3]

The praises that are lavished on Indonesia have problematic implications. Glowing declarations that Indonesia is a moderate Muslim nation or a nation where Islam and secular liberalism can successfully comingle, while they may look like compliments, are actually denigrating toward Islam. In these statements, Indonesia is portrayed as the Muslim exception: it promotes individualism, democracy, and freedom, and rejects despotism, misogyny, and irrationality—the implication being that the rest of Islam does not. The Western celebration of Indonesia is part of a culture-wars discourse that has been popularized recently where the Muslim world is divided into two types: "good" Muslims who look like "us" (Indonesia, Muslim secularists, Muslim moderates, etc.) and "bad" Muslims who oppose "us" (the Middle East, Arabs, Islamists, etc.). There is a nagging sense that the reason why "good" Muslims are "good" is that they have managed to free themselves from the tyranny of their religion. After all, in the case of Indonesia, there is a powerful idea, promoted by an older generation of anthropologists (such as Clifford Geertz), that Islam in the nation is far more relaxed than Islam elsewhere because of the enduring influence of Hinduism and Buddhism, religions that arrived in the archipelago long before Islam did.

If we really looked closely at why liberal ideals are flourishing in Indonesia, we are presented with an alternative story of power and violence in the contemporary geopolitical context. It is the story of how Muslims have embraced secular liberal ideals in spite of how the West has betrayed Indonesia time and again. In other words, secular liberal ideals are celebrated in Indonesia not because the nation is "better" than other Muslim nations, but because the previous betrayals by the West render the new promises by the West more palatable (cf. Collins 2007). The New Order, to recapitulate a foundational moment in recent Indonesian history, came into power by massacring Communists and overthrowing an incumbent left-leaning government, extraordinary acts of violence that were supported by the United States in its global efforts to promote secular democracy and curb the ideological influence of the Soviet Union. When the New Order was overthrown, Indonesians embraced democracy in hopes for a better future. Yet democratization brought about numerous deleterious effects. For example, neoliberal economic reforms that accompanied the democratization process have resulted in the destruction of Indonesian rain forests by local and foreign companies. The smoke from the illegal burning of rain forests chokes Indonesia for several months each year and creates a transnational nuisance for neighboring Malaysia, Philippines, and Singapore. Its democratically elected government, celebrated internationally for having staved off "religious" or "Islamic" violence, seems unable to solve the violence of economic liberalism.

It is thus simply untrue that Islam is the source of violence and all that is bad about the world or that Western liberalism is the source of tolerance and all that is good about the world. Other scholars have said this too. Up to the final stages of the writing of this book, I often wondered if there is virtue in repeating points that have already been made. But then something terrible happened in Bloomington, Indiana, the college town where I work and live, that changed my perspective on things. On a cool fall evening in 2015, a forty-something-year-old Muslim woman from Turkey was having tea with her nine-year-old daughter at the patio of a local café. A nineteen-year-old white male passed by drunkenly. "White power!" he yelled as he suddenly lunged toward the woman. Gripping her throat from behind, he slammed her face against the table as he tried to remove her light-blue head scarf. The woman held him off long enough for her husband, who was inside the café, and a passerby to drag the attacker away and restrain him. She was physically unhurt, but her daughter was inconsolable.

"I couldn't help you, Mommy," the young girl cried. "I couldn't help you."[4]

The attack shocked Bloomington, a progressive enclave in the middle of a conservative state. Over the next few days, members of the community organized several events to condemn such acts of violence. I attended a rally held outside the county courthouse that brought together concerned students, faculty, and local residents. The rally featured a number of speakers. One speaker, a colleague of mine whose work focuses on race and empire, spoke about how violence against Muslims in the United States was inextricably linked to the U.S. military's violence on Muslims elsewhere. In her speech, she also recounted how she had made similar arguments in a protest some twenty-five years earlier, following the U.S. invasion of Iraq in 1991 during the first Gulf War.

"I can't believe we're still protesting this shit," she said, quoting a line that is often used by social activists.

I share her dismay. Attacks on Muslims (and other brown bodies mistaken as Muslims) in the United States have escalated since September 11, 2001, to the extent that we now have a name for the rage that propels them: Islamophobia. Such acts of violence are justified by the assumptions that I am challenging in this book: that Muslims stand outside of secular liberalism, that they reject the values that "we" the West stand for, that they are set in their ways in opposing "us." Given how resilient these assumptions have proven to be, scholars concerned with the welfare of ordinary Muslims must correct these erroneous representations, tirelessly, again and again, until the violence stops.

Perhaps there is a lesson or two to be learned from Rizal, Hassan, Nuriya, and Indonesia's other experimental Muslims. They are working hard to accommodate secular liberal ideals in their religious practices, but are Western secular liberals also working to accommodate Muslims and other religious people? Our shared existence cannot be improved by putting Islam on one side and the West on the other, Muslims on one side and Western secular liberals on the other, "good" Muslims on one side and "bad" Muslims on the other, religion on one side and secularism on the other. The imaginative impasse needs to be breached.[5] Maybe this calls for improvisation and new hybrid practices.

NOTES

Prologue

1. Following ethnographic convention, I refer to my informants using pseudonyms to protect their identities. Some informants who shared certain traits or experiences were represented as composite characters in order to enhance anonymity.

Introduction

1. Amira Mittermaier (2010) studies pious Sufi Muslims in Cairo who are centrally concerned with prophetic dreams and spirit possessions. Piety is cultivated differently among them compared to the conservative Islamists of Mahmood's and Hirschkind's studies, as the Sufis not only exercise intentional action to be pious but are also acted upon by the divine or supernatural beings who appear in their dreams.

2. A good resource on the early encounters between Indonesian Muslims and modernity is James Siegel's ([1969] 2000) analysis of the modernist reform of religious thought and practice that occurred in Indonesia around the turn of the twentieth century.

3. For more detailed description and analysis on the violence committed by the New Order see, for example, the works of Benedict Anderson (2001), Edward Aspinall (2005), and James Siegel (1998).

4. The research design in Faye Ginsburg's (1998) pioneering work on the abortion debates in the United States has inspired me to examine how contestations among Muslim

ideological factions shape post–New Order Indonesia. In her work, Ginsburg examined the battles between "pro-choice" and "pro-life" activists in Fargo, North Dakota, over the presence of an abortion clinic in their city. While secular liberals frequently dismiss religious conservatives as out of touch with reality, Ginsburg importantly treats the conservatives with empathy in order to more fully represent their worldviews. Ginsburg depicts the pro-life activists not as victims of false consciousness, but as people who were concerned that the lives they led were no longer valued in a world they perceived as increasingly secular and materialist.

5. Examples of important studies on radical Islamist groups in post–New Order Indonesia are Martin van Bruinessen (2013) and Noorhaidi Hasan (2006).

6. The edited collection by Omid Safi (2003) is one such work that seeks to highlight progressive interpretations of Islam.

7. President Obama's comments about Indonesia were widely reported by the press. See, for example, Julie Hirschfeld Davis, "President Joko Widodo of Indonesia Joins Trans-Pacific Partnership," *New York Times*, October 26, 2015, https://www.nytimes.com/2015/10/27/us/politics/president-joko-widodo-of-indonesia-joins-trans-pacific-partnership.html.

8. Scholars have examined multiple aspects of the youth experience under neoliberalism. Comaroff and Comaroff (2000), for example, discuss the crisis of masculinity among male African youths, a theme that Craig Jeffrey (2010) and Pascal Menoret (2014) also explore in their works on how male youths in India and Saudi Arabia respectively cope with boredom and a lack of social mobility. Other scholars have paid attention to the female experience, such as Ritty Lukose's (2009) examination of the impact of an expanding consumer culture on young Indian women. The response to emerging youth crises is another issue that has been investigated. In her study of unemployed and underemployed Japanese youths who withdraw inward as a result of their failures to fulfil social expectations, Anne Allison (2013) observes new types of voluntary support communities that are formed to tackle these difficulties. Meanwhile, Linda Herrera's edited volume (2014) focuses on Middle Eastern youths who forge new models of civic engagement by joining online activist groups.

9. Asef Bayat (2010) offers an excellent analysis of the subversive political potential of fun and the strategies employed by conservative Islamist regimes in the Middle East to control fun activities among their youths.

10. This point has been discussed at length by scholars of religion. See, for example, Orsi 2003, 173.

11. Some anthropologists have expressed objection to the everyday Islam approach. They argue that since the approach sets itself in opposition to the self-cultivation approach, it invalidates the reality and ontology of conservative Islamists and ultimately results in a narrowing of anthropology's proper object of study (Fadil and Fernando 2015). Yet others who have defended the inclusionary potential in the everyday approach to the study of Islam point out that piety is inseparable from other domains of life, even for pious Islamists (Deeb 2015).

12. Islamic schools in Indonesia offer elementary to high school education. They tend to teach some combination of religious and secular subjects, though there are wide variations in terms of the proportion of time devoted to these subjects. Indonesians distinguish between Islamic day schools, which they call *madrasa*, and Islamic boarding schools, or *pesantren*. While the distinction between madrasa and pesantren is an important one (as they offer different curriculum, for example), it will not play a major part in this book. I will refer to all Islamic schools as madrasa.

13. The leadership of the Taliban (which in Arabic means "students") did emerge from Pakistani madrasas located near refugee camps close to the border with Afghanistan. However, the transformation of these madrasas into training centers for jihadi militants occurred at the interstices of complex political and economic factors. These madrasas grew in the

1980s following the influx of Afghan refugees into Pakistan, the lack of access to affordable education for poor Pakistanis, and donations from patrons in Pakistan, Saudi Arabia, and the Gulf states. The development of these madrasas, and subsequently the Taliban radicals they produced, were also supported by American government officials trying to cultivate support for the anti-Soviet cause. However, the intricacies behind how religious education gets entangled with radicalism are often overlooked in many post-Taliban and post-9/11 commentaries on the madrasa. For more details see Hefner and Zaman 2007.

1. The Tremblingness of Youths

1. The pamphlet's title is a reference to "Islam Yes, Partai Islam [Islamic parties] No," the famous slogan associated with the progressive Muslim leader Nurcholish Madjid. Madjid invented the slogan to express his opposition to Islamic political parties, arguing that they would reinforce exclusive identities and divide Indonesians. Instead, he believed that a secular democratic welfare state would best facilitate a good Islamic life in the sense that its socioeconomic ideals of justice and equality enabled believers to live up to their religious duties (see Künkler 2013).

2. By "tremblingness," Benedict Anderson is not referencing early twentieth-century theories relating the "storm and stress" in the lives of youths to their biological transition from childhood to adulthood (e.g., Hall 1904). Rather, Anderson demonstrates an anthropological sensibility by treating the emotional states of youths as a product of their cultural contexts.

3. Scholars of other colonial contexts have also made similar observations (e.g., Fanon [1963] 2004 on Algeria).

4. This point has also been made by numerous other scholars of Indonesia, including Hefner 2000 and Kersten 2011.

5. Population Census 2010, Statistics Indonesia (Sensus Penduduk 2010, Badan Pusat Statistik), http://sp2010.bps.go.id/index.php/site/index.

6. World Bank Data on Indonesia, http://data.worldbank.org/country/indonesia.

7. Among the numerous anthropological works on Islam that focus on education, in addition to those cited elsewhere in the book, are Eickelman 1985, Messick 1993, and Starrett 1998.

8. For a more detailed discussion of the politics of categories like "good" and "moderate" Muslims see Mahmood 2006 and Mamdani 2004.

9. Ghassan Hage (2014) makes a similar point when he describes how his colleagues expect him to "absolutely condemn" Palestinian suicide bombers when talking about them, instead of making them recognizable as human beings. But Hage argues that the denial of the humanity of suicide bombers works to turn Palestinians into abstract dehumanized others and further legitimizes Israeli colonialist invasions. Hage believes that withholding condemnation from analysis will allow scholars a better understanding of why people turn to violence: "Suicide bombings are undoubtedly a form of social evil," he argues, "but their evil is also the evil of the living conditions from which they emanate" (254).

10. A more comprehensive account of these proto-nationalist organizations can be found in Ricklefs 2002 and Shiraishi 1990.

11. The term *kaum muda* (the younger generation) was first coined in 1904 by Abdul Rivai, editor of the scholarly journal *Bintang Hindia* (Star of the Indies). Rivai defined the *kaum muda* as "all people of the Indies [young or old] who are no longer willing to follow the obsolete system [*atoeran koeno*] but are, on the contrary, anxious to achieve self-respect through knowledge and the sciences [*ilmoe*]." Rather than being a homogeneous category, the *kaum muda* was seen as representing a broad variety of people who wanted to alter the fact

of their colonial subjugation. Its opposition, the *kaum tua* (the older generation), thus represented political inertia (Latif 2008, 91–92).

12. As Benedict Anderson (1972) has argued, even though the Indonesian Revolution did not achieve important social or economic objectives for the new republic, it made morally possible the massive participation by ordinary Indonesians, especially the young, in the reconfiguration of their nation.

13. Debates about Islam and modernity at the turn of the twentieth century were enabled by the development of steamships (which enhanced travel to Mecca and Cairo, where parallel discussions on Islam and modernity were raging) and print technologies (which created the boom of Muslim periodicals in Indonesia, Malaysia, and Singapore). One prominent leader in these debates is Muhammad Natsir, a leading ideologue of the Islamist movement who began rising to prominence in the 1930s–1940s. He believed that Islam should govern all aspects of private and public affairs. But he also believed that the best way for this to be accomplished was not through a theocracy (he opposed the idea of a nation ruled by the traditionalist religious teachers) or the Islamic caliphate (its revival was thought to be unfeasible), but through a nation governed by secular politicians. Unlike secular politicians who regarded nationalism to be an end in itself, Natsir regarded nationalism as a utilitarian means of preserving Islamic values. For more details see Feener 2007 and Tagliacozzo 2013.

14. Making references to secularist Muslim leaders such as Mustafa Kamil Pasha of Egypt, Sukarno ([1927] 1970) argues that "a Moslem, wherever he may be in the Dar al-Islam [the Muslim world], is obliged by his religion to work for the welfare of the people in whose country he resides" (43). He also underscored the compatibility between Islam and Marxism, stating that "Moslems must never forget that capitalism, the enemy of Marxism, is also the enemy of Islam, since what is called surplus value in Marxist doctrine is essentially the same as usury from the Islamic standpoint" (50).

15. A sixth religion, Confucianism, was officially recognized after 2001.

16. The version of the Pancasila that included an obligation for Muslims to abide by Islamic law is known as Piagam Jakarta (Jakarta Charter).

17. The P4 program, whose full name is Penataran Pedoman Penghayatan and Pengalaman Pancasila (Guide for the Realization and Implementation of Pancasila), was in effect from 1978 till the end of the New Order. For more details see Bourchier 2015.

18. After backtracking from the Jakarta Charter, Islamist politicians subsequently adopted the new position that the Pancasila is in fact Islamic in character. Because it aims to foster unity in diversity, the Islamists argued, Pancasila is similar to the Charter of Medina, the constitution drawn in 622 CE by the Prophet Muhammad to manage the religious and tribal heterogeneity in the first Islamic community in Medina. The lesson that the Islamists have learned from this debate is that they must be able to reproduce some version of the dominant political discourses in order to avoid complete political marginalization (Muhtadi 2012).

19. Naveeda Khan (2012) observes a similar legacy of nation building in Pakistan. Khan argues that there is an aspirational quality in Pakistan's formation, which she traces to the poet, philosopher, and politician Muhammad Iqbal, considered to be the spiritual founder of the nation. From Iqbal, Pakistanis inherited an Islam with an open future: one that is directed not at achieving an ideal final form of an Islamic state, society, or self, but rather at sustaining the striving toward one. This creates a space for disputations over theological matters to rage on continuously in the nation, which can result in attempts for societal improvement as well as in violence.

20. I found it delightful that when his friends teased him about his academic tardiness, Rizal would retort, "At least I didn't take as long as Akbar Tandjung." A legendary figure in activist circles, Tandjung was a student activist in the 1960s who allegedly took eleven

years to graduate from university and who eventually became a prominent national politician (whose many appointments included the Speaker of the People's Representative Council in 1999–2004).

21. For a comparative case study of India see Jeffrey 2010.

2. Religion Unleashed

1. Similar policies were also pursued by the U.S. government during the early Cold War. The government developed a series of programs intended to cultivate religious consciousness at home and abroad to weaken the appeal of communism. For example, the government strengthened ties with the Vatican and widely distributed Bibles and other religious periodicals among Americans. In mainland Southeast Asia, the United States sent a Buddhist adviser to promote Buddhism. For more details see Hurd 2015, 68–70.

2. The party was established as the Justice Party (Partai Keadilan) in 1998 but was reconstituted as the Prosperous Justice Party in 2002. The changes were necessary because the Justice Party failed to obtain the required 2 percent electoral threshold in the 1999 elections that it needed to contest the 2004 elections. The party's performance has improved over three democratic elections in the post–New Order years: 1.4 percent of popular votes in 1999, 7.3 percent in 2004, and 7.88 percent in 2009. Its 2009 result, fourth best among over thirty competing parties, won it 57 out of 560 seats in the People's Representative Council.

3. The phrase in the original Arabic is *al-amr bi'l-ma'ruf wa 'n-nahy 'an al-munkar*.

4. Ed Husain and Maajid Nawaz are examples of authors who have written autobiographical accounts of their involvement with Islamist groups. Both of them pursued subsequent careers with think tanks concerned with countering extremism.

5. Given that their research has focused on conservative Islamists, scholars who adopt the self-cultivation approach have been uncharitably accused of legitimizing Islamist worldviews—despite their insistence that they are suspending their distaste for such groups in order to understand them in their own terms. Ali Mirsepassi and Tadd Graham Fernée (2014), for example, depicted Talal Asad as having a "romance with Islamism."

6. See also Spyer 2006 for an analysis of how the complex processes of change accompanying the fall of the New Order produced violent confrontation between Christians and Muslims in Ambon. Spyer analyses the role of the fantasy and imagination in the outbreak of violence, as people living in this unstable context struggled to figure out what was fact and what was fiction and who could be trusted and who could not.

7. When it came to power, the New Order refused to reinstate the Islamist political party Masyumi, which had been banned by the previous regime.

8. For more historical details on the reorganization of the Islamist movement during the New Order see Feener 2007 and Latif 2008.

9. Azyumardi Azra, Dina Afrianty, and Robert Hefner (2007) describe the educational reforms in Islamic universities at length.

10. Omid Safi describes the Islamist method of religious interpretation as "pamphlet Islam" or a "serious intellectual and spiritual fallacy of thinking that complex issues can be handled in four or six glossy pages" (2003, 22–23). Safi's tone is perhaps too derisive, but his point that the Islamist mode of religious practice can be somewhat reductionist or restrictive is well taken.

11. Carool Kersten's work (2011) focuses on three prominent Muslim intellectuals who emerged in the newly postcolonial era, the Algerian Mohammad Arkoun, the Egyptian Hasan Hanafi, and the Indonesian Nurcholish Madjid. According to Kersten, these scholars are progressive thinkers who have deep grounding in the Islamic heritage and attach great importance

to engaging with Islam's philosophical legacy and tradition of critical thinking. They combined their religious knowledge with recent developments in Western human sciences to engage in a double critique of both Muslim and Western discourses on Islam.

12. An article in the *New York Times* on June 25, 2000, by Jeffrey Goldberg ("Inside Jihad U.: The Education of a Holy Warrior"), for example, describes a Pakistani madrasa as a "jihad factory" that bred narrow-mindedness by teaching students exclusively Islamic subjects instead of secular subjects such as math, world history, or science. Although the article claims that "there are one million students studying in the country's 10,000 or so madrasas, and militant Islam is at the core of most of these schools," scholars like Mahmood Mamdani (2004) have argued that jihadi madrasas are not only few and far between, but were established during the Cold War by U.S. and Pakistani intelligence to create militants who could drive the Soviets out of Afghanistan.

13. Charles Kurzman conducted research on the leading and rank-and-file Islamists of the twentieth century and discovered that most attended secular schools. For example, only two of the nineteen hijackers in the 9/11 attacks attended madrasas—the rest went to secular schools. Kurzman argues that secular-educated extremists read religious scriptures by themselves instead of relying on madrasa-trained experts to understand sacred sources. Consequently, they arrive at religious ideas that depart from mainstream interpretations. Kurzman stresses that despite their opposition to the West, extremists actually embrace many modern values, as evidenced by how their goals are framed in the language of individual rights, economic development, and national self-determination. Global terrorist groups also draw on Western models of practice. Apart from copying Western tactics of combat, al-Qaeda and similar groups also "operate like transnational corporations, with affiliates and franchises, strategic partners, commodity chains, global financing, and other features associated with contemporary global capital" (Kurzman 2011, 71).

14. Diego Gambetta and Steffen Hertog (2016) examined 497 extremists in the Muslim world since the 1970s. Educational information was available for 207, of whom 93 had degrees in engineering, followed by smaller numbers of graduates of medicine, economics and business, and math and science. Like radical Islamists, violent neo-Nazis and white supremacists in the West also showed disproportionate numbers of engineers. Gambetta and Hertog theorize that engineers become radicals because of "relative deprivation," or when people's hopes for advancement are raised by higher education and then dashed by limited job prospects. They also argue that engineers are characterized by several psychological traits that are conducive to violence, including proneness to disgust (as seen, for example, in how engineers stand out in their opposition to gay rights), need for closure (their tendency to act decisively in moments of cognitive rupture), and "simplism" (the penchant to seek simple and unambiguous explanations for complicated phenomena). While Gambetta and Hertog's insights have received praise, many are less than enthused about their argument. Accusing the study of stigmatizing an entire profession, engineers are concerned that the data used by the authors are too thin and the conclusions they reached oversimplified. Another major shortcoming is that there is very little consideration for historical context in the study (for more concerns over this research see Berrett 2016).

15. The story of the prophet Lot, which appears in several parts of the Quran (e.g. 26, 169–75; 27, 54–58), is a constant referent in classical and contemporary discussions on homosexuality. According to the Quran, God sent Lot to command the people of Sodom and Gomorrah to cease their lustful and violent acts and embrace monotheism. But the tribe rejected Lot's prophecy; its men, in particular, continued to treat male strangers with inhospitality and even raped them. Having incurred God's wrath, the tribe was subsequently annihilated.

16. Anthropologists of course conducted research in Indonesia when it was still under Dutch colonial rule, as seen in the classic works of Gregory Bateson and Margaret Mead on Bali in the 1930s. The first wave of ethnographic work in independent Indonesia, led by Clifford Geertz and his contemporaries, began in the 1960s, which coincided with the rise to power of the New Order. This generation of scholars and those who followed them, according to Danilyn Rutherford (2014) and Eric Tagliacozzo (2014), studied modernity, globalization, and power, but instead observed strange occurrences such as ghosts, magical beings, and other things that do not fit neatly into modern rational categories. Rutherford and Tagliacozzo attribute these unrecognizable entities to the techniques of rule employed by the New Order.

3. Accounting for the Soul

1. The accounting notebook is similar to the *buku solat* (prayer book) that is used in madrasas to encourage children to keep up with their religious rituals. The Islamists use the notebook in a slightly different way, as it functions as a technology of discipline for young adults and is understood in relation to the contemporary political discourse of transparency.

2. The phrase in the original Indonesian is *hitunglah amal kita sebelum hari perhitungan itu tiba*.

3. The Campus Proselytization Association chapter at the University of Indonesia had approximately two hundred participants, with roughly equal numbers of men and women.

4. For a useful summary on the advent of neoliberalism in Indonesia see Luvaas 2012.

5. Sahih al-Bukhari, vol. 7, book 72, no. 674.

6. Sahih al-Bukhari, vol. 7, book 72, no. 781.

7. The interview took place in Jakarta on February 11, 2009.

8. See Bowen 1993, 24, on Indonesian debates on sincerity.

4. Playing with Scriptures

1. Among the numerous works focusing on progressive Muslims in Indonesia, in addition to those discussed elsewhere in the book, are Lukens-Bull 2005 and Robinson 2008.

2. An authoritative compilation of writings by modernist Muslim thinkers is Kurzman 2002.

3. Works that have paid careful attention to the important place of debates in Islamic education include Gilsenan (1982) 2005, Hefner and Zaman 2007, and Zaman 2007.

4. For a definitive list of fiqh texts used in Islamic schools in Indonesia see Bruinessen 1990.

5. Ethnographic descriptions of the importance of self study in Islamic schools across cultural contexts can be found in Dhofier (1982) 1999 (Indonesia), Eickelman 1978 (Morocco), and Messick 1993 (Yemen).

6. The speech has been reproduced in Madjid 1987. For a more detailed analysis of Madjid's arguments on religion and politics see Kersten 2011.

7. Fischer 1980 offers an excellent ethnographic account of the pedagogy of the ayatollahs of Iran.

8. The *Republik Mimpi* program was eventually canceled in 2008, but it led to the birth of many other political satire television programs, including *Democrazy, Sentilan Sentilun,* and *Provocative Proactive.*

9. Ani Yudhoyono, wife of President Susilo Bambang Yudhoyono (2004–2014), was a recent target of online mockery. Internet users criticized Mrs. Yudhoyono for putting up

pictures of her opulent lifestyle on the Instagram photo-sharing site, arguing that such behavior was inappropriate for the First Lady. Mrs. Yudhoyono lashed out at her critics, who then retaliated by creating memes mocking her anger, including one memorably captioned "Istana-geram," or the angry (presidential) palace, a play on the word "Instagram."

10. A useful biography of Abdurrahman Wahid can be found on Encyclopaedia Britannica, http://www.britannica.com/biography/Abdurrahman-Wahid.

11. See Barton 2002 for more details.

12. There has been extensive discussion among scholars of Islam of Muhammad's marriages, including the controversial marriage to Aisha. For a useful summary of the debates over the marriages see J. Brown 2011.

13. The Indonesian name of this organization is Aliansi Kebangsaan untuk Kebebasan Beragama dan Berkeyakinan, or AKKBB for short.

14. Q 33, 59.

15. Q 24, 31.

5. From Moderate Indonesia to Indonistan

1. For more details on contemporary efforts by Western policy makers to promote religious freedom across the globe see Sullivan et al. 2015. The book unsettles the widely held assumption that religious freedom is a necessary condition for peace and demonstrates that the reasons for violence and discrimination are often more complex than acknowledged in policy-making circles.

2. Haeril Halim, "Congresses to Promote Moderate View of Islam," *Jakarta Post*, July 31, 2015, http://www.thejakartapost.com/news/2015/07/31/congresses-promote-moderate-view-islam.html.

3. Hyginus Hardoyo, "The Week in Review: Moderate Islam in Indonesia," *Jakarta Post*, August 9, 2015, http://www.thejakartapost.com/news/2015/08/09/the-week-review-moderate-islam-indonesia.html.

4. Joe Cochrane, "From Indonesia, a Muslim Challenge to the Ideology of the Islamic State," *New York Times*, November 26, 2015, https://www.nytimes.com/2015/11/27/world/asia/indonesia-islam-nahdlatul-ulama.html.

5. A Jakarta-based nongovernmental organization, the Liberal Islam Network (Jaringan Islam Liberal) promotes the discourse of liberal Islam through its publications and public events and attracts many youth participants from student organizations such as Formaci. Although it is not the only promoter of liberal Islam in Indonesia, the Liberal Islam Network has often been singled out for criticism by conservative forces.

6. The Wahid Institute, another Jakarta-based rights monitoring group, similarly noted an increase in the number of cases that are based on religious biases. It documented 92 violations of religious freedom and 184 incidents of religious intolerance in 2011, up from 64 violations and 134 incidents of intolerance in 2010.

7. Prashanth Parameswaran, "Is Indonesia Really the World's Most Tolerant Muslim Country?," *Diplomat*, December 30, 2014, https://thediplomat.com/2014/12/is-indonesia-really-the-worlds-most-tolerant-muslim-country/.

8. Andreas Harsono, "No Model for Muslim Democracy," *New York Times*, May 21, 2012, http://www.nytimes.com/2012/05/22/opinion/no-model-for-muslim-democracy.html.

9. Anda Bertanya, Habib Rizieq Menjawab, https://www.facebook.com/habib.men jawab/.

10. Seth Mydans, "The World: Secular Rules; In Indonesia, Islamic Politics Doesn't Mean Religion," *New York Times*, October 24, 1999, http://www.nytimes.com/1999/10/24/weekin review/the-world-secular-rules-in-indonesia-islamic-politics-doesn-t-mean-religion.html.

11. Scholars have argued that challenges to the Suharto-era discourses on women came largely from the civil society and not from the government of Megawati Sukarnoputri, Indonesia's first female president (2001–2004). President Sukarnoputri's policies were so rarely concerned with women's issues that Indonesian feminists refused to acknowledge her as a kindred spirit (Brenner 2006).

12. For a useful ethnographic account of the activities organized by Islamist women in Indonesia see Rinaldo 2013.

13. I am echoing the point made by Lila Abu-Lughod (2013), who criticizes the U.S. invasion of Afghanistan in 2001 on the pretext of liberating Afghan women from the burqa. Abu-Lughod argues that the notion that all women want the individual freedom envisioned by Western feminism is simply misguided. "Might other desires be meaningful for people? Might living in close families be more valued? Living in a godly way? Living without war? I have done ethnographic work in Egypt for more than thirty years and I cannot think of a single woman I know . . . who has expressed envy of women in the United States, women they variously perceive as bereft of community, cut off from family, vulnerable to sexual violence and social anomie, driven by selfishness or individual success, subject to capitalist pressures, participants in imperial ventures that don't respect the sovereignty and intelligence of others, or strangely disrespectful of others and God" (45).

14. An example is Q 24, 30–31. The verse begins with "Say to the believing men that they should lower their gaze and guard their modesty / That will make for greater purity for them / And Allah is well acquainted with all that they do / And say to the believing women that they should lower their gaze and guard their modesty."

15. Some important analyses of Muslim discourses on the husband's rights over the wife include Chaudhry 2013 and Fadl 2006.

16. Additional details on the Islamist matchmaking process in Indonesia can be found in Smith-Hefner 2005.

17. Hans Nicholas Jong, "National Police Confirms Virginity Tests for Female Candidates," *Jakarta Post*, November 19, 2014.

18. My attempts to disrupt the connections that have often been made between Islam and violence are influenced by Michael Gilsenan's masterly analysis of violence in Lebanon (1996). Gilsenan conducted fieldwork in the 1970s just before the outbreak of the Lebanese civil war. Though his research focused on a Sunni Muslim part of the country, Islam is conspicuously absent in the ethnography. Instead, Gilsenan describes a highly stratified society where the big landowners use the small landowners as henchmen to control the laborers at the bottom of the hierarchy and as proxies to compete for social prestige with the other great lords. Patriarchy and the honor of men are at the center of this society, as brute strength becomes a central metaphor for rule, power is attained through violent competition, women are powerless to resist sexual exploitation, and the social pecking order is displayed by humiliating one's social inferiors. Gilsenan thus depicts a society in which violence is an attribute not of religion (specifically Islam) but of toxic masculinity.

Epilogue

1. "Text: Obama's Speech in Cairo," *New York Times*, June 4, 2009, http://www.nytimes.com/2009/06/04/us/politics/04obama.text.html.

2. Mark Landler, "Clinton Praises Indonesian Democracy," *New York Times*, February 18, 2009, http://www.nytimes.com/2009/02/19/washington/19diplo.html.

3. Nicholas Watt, "Cameron Calls on Islam to Embrace Democracy and Reject Extremism," *Guardian*, April 12, 2012, https://www.theguardian.com/world/2012/apr/12/cameron-islam-embrace-democracy-extremism.

4. Annie Garau, "Bloomington Resident Reflects on Racially Triggered Assault," *Indiana Daily Student*, October 19, 2015, http://www.idsnews.com/article/2015/10/bloomington-resident-reflects-on-racially-triggered-assault.

5. I borrow the phrase "imaginative impasse" from Hannah Appel (2014), who uses it to describe the work put in by the Occupy Wall Street activists to overcome the staleness of ideas associated with the current global economy and propose new ways of imagining how the economy should function.

BIBLIOGRAPHY

Abu-Lughod, Lila. 2013. *Do Muslim Women Need Saving?* Cambridge, MA: Harvard University Press.

Agrama, Hussein Ali. 2012. *Questioning Secularism: Islam, Sovereignty, and the Rule of Law in Modern Egypt*. Chicago: University of Chicago Press.

Allison, Anne. 2013. *Precarious Japan*. Durham, NC: Duke University Press.

Anderson, Benedict. 1972. *Java in a Time of Revolution: Occupation and Resistance, 1944–1946*. Ithaca, NY: Cornell University Press.

———. 1983. *Imagined Communities: Reflections on the Origins and Spread of Nationalism*. London: Verso.

———. 1990. *Language and Power: Exploring Political Cultures in Indonesia*. Ithaca, NY: Cornell University Press.

———, ed. 2001. *Violence and the State in Suharto's Indonesia*. Ithaca, NY: Cornell University Press.

Appel, Hannah. 2014. "Occupy Wall Street and the Economic Imagination." *Cultural Anthropology* 29 (4): 602–25.

Asad, Talal. 1986. *The Idea of an Anthropology of Islam*. Washington, DC: Center for Contemporary Arab Studies.

———. 1993. *Genealogies of Religion: Discipline and Reasons of Power in Christianity and Islam*. Baltimore: Johns Hopkins University Press.

——. 2003. *Formations of the Secular: Christianity, Islam and Modernity*. Stanford, CA: Stanford University Press.

Aspinall, Edward. 2005. *Opposing Suharto: Compromise, Resistance, and Regime Change in Indonesia*. Stanford, CA: Stanford University Press.

Azra, Azyumardi, Dina Afrianty, and Robert Hefner. 2007. "Pesantren and Madrasa: Muslim Schools and National Ideals in Indonesia." In *Schooling Islam: The Culture and Politics of Modern Muslim Education*, edited by R. Hefner and M. Q. Zaman, 172–98. Princeton, NJ: Princeton University Press.

Barton, Greg. 2002. *Abdurrahman Wahid: Muslim Democrat, Indonesian President*. Honolulu: University of Hawai'i Press.

Bayat, Asef. 2010. *Life as Politics: How Ordinary People Can Change the Middle East*. Stanford, CA: Stanford University Press.

Berrett, Dan. 2016. "The Dangers of Certainty." In *Chronicle of Higher Education* 62 (29): B6–9.

Boellstorff, Tom. 2005. *The Gay Archipelago: Sexuality and Nation in Indonesia*. Princeton, NJ: Princeton University Press.

Bohannan, Laura. 1966. "Shakespeare in the Bush: An American Anthropologist Set Out to Study the Tiv of West Africa and Was Taught the True Meaning of *Hamlet*." *Natural History* 75:28–33.

Bourchier, David. 2015. *Illiberal Democracy in Indonesia: The Ideology of the Family State*. New York: Routledge.

Bowen, John. 1993. *Muslims through Discourse*. Princeton, NJ: Princeton University Press.

——. 2003. *Islam, Law, and Equality in Indonesia: An Anthropology of Public Reasoning*. Cambridge: Cambridge University Press.

Boyarin, Jonathan, ed. 1993. *The Ethnography of Reading*. Berkeley: University of California Press.

Brenner, Suzanne. 2006. "Democracy, Polygamy, and Women in Post-Reformasi Indonesia." *Social Analysis* 50 (1): 164–70.

Brown, Jonathan. 2011. *Muhammad: A Very Short Introduction*. Oxford: Oxford University Press.

Brown, Wendy. 2009. Introduction to *Is Critique Secular? Blasphemy, Injury, and Free Speech*, edited by T. Asad, W. Brown, J. Butler, and S. Mahmood, 1–19. Berkeley: University of California Press.

Bruinessen, Martin van. 1990. "Kitab Kuning: Books in Arabic Script Used in the Pesantren Milieu." *Bijdragen tot de Taal-, Land- en Volkenkunde* 146 (2/3): 226–69.

——, ed. 2013. *Contemporary Developments in Indonesian Islam: Explaining the "Conservative Turn."* Singapore: ISEAS.

Budiman, Manneke. 2008. "Treading the Path of the Shari'a: Indonesian Feminism at the Crossroads of Western Modernity and Islamism." *Journal of Indonesian Social Sciences and Humanities* 1:73–93.

Certeau, Michel de. 1984. *The Practice of Everyday Life*. Berkeley: University of California Press.

Chartier, Roger. 1994. *The Order of Books*. Translated by L. Cochrane. Cambridge: Polity.

Chaudhry, Ayesha. 2013. *Domestic Violence and the Islamic Tradition: Ethics, Law and the Muslim Discourse on Gender*. Oxford: Oxford University Press.

Collins, Elizabeth Fuller. 2007. *Indonesia Betrayed: How Development Fails*. Honolulu: University of Hawai'i Press.

Comaroff, Jean, and John Comaroff. 2000. "Millennial Capitalism: First Thoughts on a Second Coming." *Public Culture* 12 (2): 291–343.

Deeb, Lara. 2006. *An Enchanted Modern: Gender and Public Piety in Shi'i Lebanon*. Princeton, NJ: Princeton University Press.

———. 2015. "Thinking Piety and the Everyday Together: A Response to Fadil and Fernando." *HAU: Journal of Ethnographic Theory* 5 (2): 93–96.

Deeb, Lara, and Mona Harb. 2013. *Leisurely Islam: Negotiating Geography and Morality in Shi'ite South Beirut*. Princeton, NJ: Princeton University Press.

Dhofier, Zamakhsyari. (1982) 1999. *The Pesantren Tradition: The Role of the Kyai in the Maintenance of Traditional Islam in Java*. Tempe, AZ: Program for Southeast Asian Studies, Arizona State University.

Doorn-Harder, Pieternella van. 2006. *Women Shaping Islam: Indonesian Women Reading the Quran*. Urbana: University of Illinois Press.

Durkheim, Émile. (1912) 1995. *The Elementary Forms of Religious Life*. New York: Free Press.

Eickelman, Dale. 1978. "The Art of Memory: Islamic Education and Its Social Reproduction." *Comparative Studies in Society and History* 20 (4): 485–516.

———. 1985. *Knowledge and Power in Morocco: The Education of a Twentieth-Century Notable*. Princeton, NJ: Princeton University Press.

Eickelman, Dale, and Jon Anderson, eds. 1999. *New Media in the Muslim World: The Emerging Public Sphere*. Bloomington: Indiana University Press.

Eickelman, Dale, and James Piscatori. 1996. *Muslim Politics*. Princeton, NJ: Princeton University Press.

Fadil, Nadia, and Mayanthi Fernando. 2015. "Rediscovering the 'Everyday' Muslim: Notes on an Anthropological Divide." *HAU: Journal of Ethnographic Theory* 5 (2): 59–88.

Fadl, Khaled Abou El. 2006. *Conference of the Books*. Lanham, MD: Rowman & Littlefield.

Fanon, Frantz. (1963) 2004. *The Wretched of the Earth*. New York: Grove.

Farsad, Negin, and Dean Obeidallah, dirs. 2013. *The Muslims Are Coming!* 81 min.

Feener, R. Michael. 2007. *Muslim Legal Thought in Modern Indonesia*. Cambridge: Cambridge University Press.

Ferguson, James, and Akhil Gupta. 2002. "Spatializing States: Toward an Ethnography of Neoliberal Governmentality." *American Ethnologist* 29 (4): 981–1002.

Fischer, Michael. 1980. *Iran: From Religious Dispute to Revolution*. Cambridge, MA: Harvard University Press.

Fischer, Michael, and Mehdi Abedi. 1990. *Debating Muslims: Cultural Dialogues in Postmodernity and Tradition*. Madison: University of Wisconsin Press.

Foucault, Michel. 1988. "Technologies of the Self." In *Technologies of the Self: A Seminar with Michel Foucault*, edited by M. Luther, H. Gutman, and P. Hutton, 16–49. Amherst: University of Massachusetts Press.

Foulcher, Keith. 2000. "Sumpah Pemuda: The Making and Meaning of a Symbol of In-donesian Nationhood." *Asian Studies Review* 24 (3): 377–410.

Gade, Anna. 2004. *Perfection Makes Practice: Learning, Emotion, and the Recited Qur'an in Indonesia*. Honolulu: University of Hawai'i Press.

Gambetta, Diego, and Steffen Hertog. 2016. *Engineers of Jihad: The Curious Connection between Violent Extremism and Education*. Princeton, NJ: Princeton University Press.

Geertz, Clifford. 1968. *Islam Observed: Religious Development in Morocco and Indo-nesia*. New Haven, CT: Yale University Press.

———. 1973. *The Interpretation of Cultures*. New York: Basic Books.

Gerth, H. H., and C. Wright Mills. 1946. *From Max Weber: Essays in Sociology*. New York: Oxford University Press.

Gilsenan, Michael. (1982) 2005. *Recognizing Islam: Religion and Society in the Mod-ern Middle East*. New York: I. B. Tauris.

———. 1996. *Lords of the Lebanese Marches: Violence and Narrative in an Arab Society*. Berkeley: University of California Press.

Ginsburg, Faye. 1998. *Contested Lives: The Abortion Debate in an American Commu-nity*. Berkeley: University of California Press.

Goffman, Erving. (1959) 1990. *The Presentation of Self in Everyday Life*. New York: Anchor Books.

Goldman, Michael. 2007. "How 'Water for All!' Policy Became Hegemonic: The Power of the World Bank and Its Transnational Policy Networks." *Geoforum* 38 (5): 786–800.

Goody, Jack, ed. 1968. *Literacy in Traditional Societies*. Cambridge: Cambridge University Press.

Guyer, Jane. 2013. " 'The Quickening of the Unknown': Epistemologies of Surprise in Anthropology." *HAU: Journal of Ethnographic Theory* 3 (3): 283–307.

Habermas, Jürgen. 1962. *The Structural Transformation of the Public Sphere: An In-quiry into a Category of Bourgeois Society*. Cambridge: Polity.

Hage, Ghassan. 2014. "Understanding Suicide Bombers." In *Moral Anthropology: A Critical Reader*, edited by D. Fassin and S. Leze, 249–55. New York: Routledge.

Hall, G. Stanley. 1904. *Adolescence: Its Psychology and Its Relations to Physiology, An-thropology, Sociology, Sex, Crime, Religion and Education*. New York: D. Appleton.

Hallam, Elizabeth, and Tim Ingold, eds. 2007. *Creativity and Cultural Improvisation*. Oxford: Berg.

Harding, Susan. 2000. *The Book of Jerry Falwell: Fundamentalist Language and Poli-tics*. Princeton, NJ: Princeton University Press.

Harvey, David. 2005. *A Brief History of Neoliberalism*. Oxford: Oxford University Press.

Hasan, Noorhaidi. 2006. *Laskar Jihad: Islam, Militancy, and the Quest for Identity in Post–New Order Indonesia*. Ithaca, NY: Cornell University Press.

———. 2009. "Islamist Party, Electoral Politics and Da'wa Mobilization among Youth: The Prosperous Justice Party (PKS) in Indonesia." RSIS Working Paper No. 184.

Hefner, Robert. 2000. *Civil Islam: Muslims and Democratization in Indonesia*. Prince-ton, NJ: Princeton University Press.

———. 2009. "Islamic Schools, Social Movements, and Democracy in Indonesia." In *Making Modern Muslims: The Politics of Islamic Education in Southeast Asia*, edited by R. Hefner, 55–105. Honolulu: University of Hawai'i Press.

Hefner, Robert, and Patricia Horvatich, eds. 1997. *Islam in an Era of Nation-States: Politics and Religious Revival in Muslim Southeast Asia*. Honolulu: University of Hawai'i Press.

Hefner, Robert, and Muhammad Qasim Zaman, eds. 2007. *Schooling Islam: The Culture and Politics of Modern Muslim Education*. Princeton, NJ: Princeton University Press.

Herrera, Linda, ed. 2014. *Wired Citizenship: Youth Learning and Activism in the Middle East*. New York: Routledge.

Herzfeld, Michael. 2004. *The Body Impolitic: Artisans and Artifice in the Global Hierarchy of Value*. Chicago: University of Chicago Press.

———. 2005. *Cultural Intimacy: Social Poetics in the Nation-State*. New York: Routledge.

Hirschkind, Charles. 2006. *The Ethical Soundscape: Cassette Sermons and Islamic Counterpublics*. New York: Columbia University Press.

Hoesterey, James. 2016. *Rebranding Islam: Piety, Prosperity, and a Self-Help Guru*. Stanford, CA: Stanford University Press.

Huizinga, Johan. 1950. *Homo Ludens: A Study of the Play Element in Culture*. New York: Roy Publishers.

Huntington, Samuel. 1996. *The Clash of Civilizations and the Remaking of World Order*. New York: Simon & Schuster.

Hurd, Elizabeth. 2015. *Beyond Religious Freedom: The New Global Politics of Religion*. Princeton, NJ: Princeton University Press.

Ibrahim, Nur Amali. 2015. "The Problem with the 'Moderate Muslim' Label." Spring Forum, Consortium for the Study of Religion, Ethics, and Society, Indiana University. https://csres.iu.edu/pages/forum-folder/forumspring2015.php.

———. 2016. "Homophobic Muslims: Emerging Trends in Multireligious Singapore." *Comparative Studies in Society and History* 58 (4): 955–81.

Jahroni, Jajang. 2004. "Defending the Majesty of Islam: Indonesia's Front Pembela Islam (FPI), 1998–2003." *Studia Islamika* 11 (2): 197–256.

Jeffrey, Craig. 2010. *Timepass: Youth, Class, and the Politics of Waiting in India*. Stanford, CA: Stanford University Press.

Jones, Carla. 2007. "Fashion and Faith in Urban Indonesia." *Fashion Theory* 11 (2/3): 211–32.

Keane, Webb. 2009. "Freedom and Blasphemy: On Indonesian Press Bans and Danish Cartoons." *Public Culture* 21 (1): 47–76.

Kersten, Carool. 2011. *Cosmopolitan and Heretics: New Muslim Intellectuals and the Study of Islam*. New York: Columbia University Press.

Khan, Naveeda. 2012. *Muslim Becoming: Aspiration and Skepticism in Pakistan*. Durham, NC: Duke University Press.

Kugle, Scott. 2010. *Homosexuality in Islam: Critical Reflection on Gay, Lesbian and Transgender Muslims*. Oxford: Oneworld.

Kulick, Don. 2010. "Humorless Lesbians." In *Femininity, Feminism and Gendered Discourse: A Selected and Edited Collection of Papers from the Fifth International*

Language and Gender Association Conference (IGALAS), edited by J. Holmes and M. Marra, 59–81. Newcastle upon Tyne: Cambridge Scholars.

Künkler, Mirjam. 2013. "How Pluralist Democracy Became the Consensual Discourse among Secular and Nonsecular Muslims in Indonesia." In *Democracy and Islam in Indonesia*, edited by M. Künkler and A. Stepan, 53–72. New York: Columbia University Press.

Kurzman, Charles, ed. 1998. *Liberal Islam*. Oxford: Oxford University Press.

——, ed. 2002. *Modernist Islam, 1840–1940: A Sourcebook*. New York: Oxford University Press.

——. 2011. *The Missing Martyrs: Why There Are So Few Muslim Terrorists*. New York: Oxford University Press.

Lambek, Michael. 1993. *Knowledge and Practice in Mayotte: Local Discourses of Islam, Sorcery, and Spirit Possession*. Toronto: University of Toronto Press.

Lane, Max. 2008. *Unfinished Nation: Indonesia before and after Suharto*. London: Verso.

Latif, Yudi. 2008. *Indonesian Muslim Intelligentsia and Power*. Singapore: Institute of Southeast Asian Studies.

Lave, Jean, and Étienne Wenger. 1991. *Situated Learning: Legitimate Peripheral Participation*. Cambridge: Cambridge University Press.

Lee, Doreen. 2016. *Activist Archives: Youth Culture and the Political Past in Indonesia*. Durham, NC: Duke University Press.

Lent, John. 2015. *Asian Comics*. Jackson: University Press of Mississippi.

Li, Tania. 2007. *The Will to Improve: Governmentality, Development, and the Practice of Politics*. Durham, NC: Duke University Press.

Livingston, Julie. 2012. *Improvising Medicine: An African Oncology Ward in an Emerging Cancer Epidemic*. Durham, NC: Duke University Press.

Lukens-Bull, Ronald. 2005. *A Peaceful Jihad: Negotiating Identity and Modernity in Muslim Java*. New York: Palgrave Macmillan.

Lukose, Ritty. 2009. *Liberalization's Children: Gender, Youth, and Consumer Citizenship in Globalizing India*. Durham, NC: Duke University Press.

Luvaas, Brent. 2012. *DIY: Style Fashion, Music and Global Digital Cultures*. London: Berg.

Madjid, Nurcholish. (1970) 1987. *Keharusan Pembaruan Pemikiran Islam dan Masalah Integrasi Umat* [The need for renewing Islamic thought and the problems of the integration of the Muslim community]. Bandung: Mizan.

Mahmood, Saba. 2005. *Politics of Piety: The Islamic Revival and the Feminist Subject*. Princeton, NJ: Princeton University Press.

——. 2006. "Secularism, Hermeneutics, and Empire: The Politics of Islamic Reformation." *Public Culture* 18 (2): 323–47.

——. 2009. "Religious Reason and Secular Affect: An Incommensurable Divide?" In *Is Critique Secular? Blasphemy, Injury, and Free Speech*, edited by T. Asad, W. Brown, J. Butler, and S. Mahmood, 64–100. Berkeley: University of California Press.

Mamdani, Mahmood. 2004. *Good Muslim, Bad Muslim: America, the Cold War, and the Roots of Terror*. New York: Pantheon Books.

Mannheim, Karl. 1952. "The Problem of Generations." In *Essays on the Sociology of Knowledge*, edited by K. Mannheim, 378–404. New York: Oxford University Press.

Marsden, Magnus. 2005. *Living Islam: Muslim Religious Experience in Pakistan's North-West Frontier*. Cambridge: Cambridge University Press.

Marx, Karl. (1867) 1992. *Capital*. Vol. 1, *A Critique of Political Economy*. London: Penguin Classics.

Massad, Joseph. 2015. *Islam in Liberalism*. Chicago: University of Chicago Press.

Masud, Muhammad Khalid, Brinkley Messick, and David Powers, eds. 1996. *Islamic Legal Interpretation: Muftis and Their Fatwas*. Cambridge, MA: Harvard University Press.

Mauss, Marcel. (1923) 2000. *The Gift: The Form and Reason for Exchange in Archaic Societies*. New York: W. W. Norton.

Menoret, Pascal. 2014. *Joyriding in Riyadh: Oil, Urbanism, and Road Revolt*. New York: Cambridge University Press.

Merry, Sally Engle. 2011. "Measuring the World: Indicators, Human Rights, and Global Governance." *Current Anthropology* 52 (S3): S83–95.

———. 2016. *The Seductions of Quantification: Measuring Human Rights, Gender Violence, and Sex Trafficking*. Chicago: University of Chicago Press.

Messick, Brinkley. 1993. *The Calligraphic State: Textual Domination and History in a Muslim Society*. Berkeley: University of California Press.

Mirsepassi, Ali, and Tadd Graham Fernée. 2014. *Islam, Democracy, and Cosmopolitanism: At Home and in the World*. Cambridge: Cambridge University Press.

Mittermaier, Amira. 2010. *Dreams That Matter: Egyptian Landscapes of the Imagination*. Berkeley: University of California Press.

———. 2013. "Trading with God: Islam, Calculation, Excess." In *A Companion to the Anthropology of Religion*, edited by J. Boddy and M. Lambek, 274–93. Chichester, West Sussex, UK: Wiley Blackwell.

Muhtadi, Burhanuddin. 2006. *Islamisme, PKS, dan Representasi Politik Perempuan* [Islamism, PKS, and the representations of women's politics]. Jakarta: Jaringan Islam Liberal.

———. 2012. *Dilema PKS: Suara dan Syariah* [The dilemmas of PKS: Popular support and sharia law]. Jakarta: Gramedia.

Ong, Aihwa, and Stephen Collier, eds. 2005. *Global Assemblages: Technology, Politics, and Ethics as Anthropological Problems*. Malden, MA: Blackwell.

Orsi, Robert A. 2003. "Is the Study of Lived Religion Irrelevant to the World We Live In?" Special presidential plenary address, Society for the Scientific Study of Religion, Salt Lake City, November 2, 2002. *Journal for the Scientific Study of Religion* 42 (2): 169–74.

———. 2012. "Afterword: Everyday Religion and the Contemporary World; The Un-Modern, or What Was Supposed to Have Disappeared but Did Not." In *Ordinary Lives and Grand Schemes: An Anthropology of Everyday Religion*, edited by J. S. Schielke and L. Debevec, 146–60. New York: Berghahn Books.

Paramaditha, Intan. 2007. "*Pasir Berbisik* and New Women's Aesthetics in Indonesian Cinema." *Jump Cut: A Review of Contemporary Media* 49 (Spring 2007).

———. 2014. "Tracing Frictions in the Act of Killing." *Film Quarterly* 67 (2): 44–49.

———. 2015. "*Spinner of Darkness*" and Other Tales. Jakarta: Lontar.

Pemberton, John. 1994. *On the Subject of "Java."* Ithaca, NY: Cornell University Press.

Poovey, Mary. 1998. *A History of the Modern Fact: Problems of Knowledge in the Sciences of Wealth and Society*. Chicago: University of Chicago Press.

Porter, Theodore. 1995. *Trust in Numbers: The Pursuit of Objectivity in Science and Public Life*. Princeton, NJ: Princeton University Press.

Rancière, Jacques. 1991. *The Ignorant Schoolmaster: Five Lessons in Intellectual Emancipation*. Translated by K. Ross. Stanford, CA: Stanford University Press.

Ricklefs, M. C. 2002. *A History of Modern Indonesia since C. 1200*. Stanford, CA: Stanford University Press.

Rinaldo, Rachel. 2013. *Mobilizing Piety: Islam and Feminism in Indonesia*. New York: Oxford University Press.

Robinson, Kathryn. 2008. *Gender, Islam and Democracy in Indonesia*. New York: Routledge.

Rose, Nikolas. 1999. *Powers of Freedom: Reframing Political Thought*. Cambridge: Cambridge University Press.

Rosenberg, Daniel, and Susan Harding. 2005. *Histories of the Future*. Durham, NC: Duke University Press.

Rudnyckyj, Daromir. 2004. "Technologies of Servitude: Governmentality and Indonesian Transnational Labor Migration." *Anthropological Quarterly* 77 (3): 407–34.

——. 2010. *Spiritual Economies: Islam, Globalization, and the Afterlife of Development*. Ithaca, NY: Cornell University Press.

Rutherford, Danilyn. 2014. "Both Places at Once." In *Producing Indonesia: The State of the Field of Indonesia Studies*, edited by E. Tagliacozzo, 25–32. Ithaca, NY: Cornell Southeast Asia Program Publications.

Ryter, Loren. 1998. "Pemuda Pancasila: The Last Loyalist Free Men of Suharto's Order." *Indonesia* 66 (October 1998): 45–73.

Safi, Omid, ed. 2003. *Progressive Muslims: On Justice, Gender, and Pluralism*. Oxford: Oneworld.

Said, Edward. 1979. *Orientalism*. New York: Vintage.

Schielke, Samuli. 2015. *Egypt in the Future Tense: Hope, Frustration, and Ambivalence before and after 2011*. Bloomington: Indiana University Press.

Sensus Penduduk 2010. Badan Pusat Statistik [Population Census 2010, Statistics Indonesia]. http://sp2010.bps.go.id/index.php/site/index.

Shiraishi, Takashi. 1990. *An Age in Motion: Popular Radicalism in Java, 1912–1926*. Ithaca, NY: Cornell University Press.

Siegel, James. (1969) 2000. *The Rope of God*. Ann Arbor: University of Michigan Press.

——. 1998. *A New Criminal Type in Jakarta: Counter-revolution Today*. Durham, NC: Duke University Press.

——. 2006. *Naming the Witch*. Cultural Memory in the Present. Stanford, CA: Stanford University Press.

Smith-Hefner, Nancy. 2005. "The New Muslim Romance: Changing Patterns of Courtship and Marriage among Educated Javanese Youth." *Journal of Southeast Asian Studies* 36 (3): 441–59.

Spyer, Patricia. 2006. "Some Notes on Disorder in the Indonesian Postcolony." In *Law and Disorder in the Postcolony*, edited by J. Comaroff and J. Comaroff, 188–218. Chicago: University of Chicago Press.

——. 2014. "After Violence—a Discussion." In *Producing Indonesia: The State of the Field of Indonesian Studies*, edited by E. Tagliacozzo, 47–62. Ithaca, NY: Cornell Southeast Asia Program Publications.

Starrett, Gregory. 1998. *Putting Islam to Work: Education, Politics, and Religious Transformation in Egypt*. Berkeley: University of California Press.

Steedly, Mary. 2013a. *Rifle Reports: A Story of Indonesian Independence*. Berkeley: University of California Press.

——. 2013b. "Transparency and Apparition: Media Ghosts of Post–New Order Indonesia." In *Images That Move*, edited by P. Spyer and M. Steedly, 257–94. Santa Fe, NM: School for Advanced Research Press.

Strassler, Karen. 2010. *Refracted Visions: Popular Photography and National Modernity in Java*. Durham, NC: Duke University Press.

Strathern, Marilyn, ed. 2000. *Audit Cutures: Anthropological Studies in Accountability, Ethics and the Academy*. London: Routledge.

Sukarno. (1927) 1970. *Nationalism, Islam, and Marxism*. Translated by K. H. Warouw and P. D. Weldon. Ithaca, NY: Modern Indonesia Project, Cornell University.

Sullivan, Winnifred Fallers. 2005. *The Impossibility of Religious Freedom*. Princeton, NJ: Princeton University Press.

Sullivan, Winnifred, Elizabeth Shakman Hurd, Saba Mahmood, and Peter G. Danchin, eds. 2015. *Politics of Religious Freedom*. Chicago: University of Chicago Press.

Tagliacozzo, Eric. 2013. *The Longest Journey: Southeast Asians and the Pilgrimage to Mecca*. Oxford: Oxford University Press.

——, ed. 2014. *Producing Indonesia: The State of the Field of Indonesian Studies*. Ithaca, NY: Cornell Southeast Asia Program Publications.

Tobin, Sarah. 2016. *Everyday Piety: Islam and Economy in Jordan*. Ithaca, NY: Cornell University Press.

Tsing, Anna. 2005. *Friction: An Ethnography of Global Connection*. Princeton, NJ: Princeton University Press.

Tuchman, Gaye. 2009. *Wannabe U: Inside the Corporate University*. Chicago: University of Chicago Press.

Weintraub, Andrew, ed. 2011. *Islam and Popular Culture in Indonesia and Malaysia*. Abingdon, Oxon, UK: Routledge.

Welker, Marina. 2014. *Enacting the Corporation: An American Mining Firm in Post-authoritarian Indonesia*. Berkeley: University of California Press.

Wieringa, Saskia. 2003. 'The Birth of the New Order State in Indonesia: Sexual Politics and Nationalism." *Journal of Women's History* 15 (1): 70–92.

World Bank. 2017. Indonesia data. http://data.worldbank.org/country/indonesia.

Zaman, Muhammad Qasim. 2007. *The Ulama in Contemporary Islam: Custodians of Change*. Princeton, NJ: Princeton University Press.

INDEX